A GRIM ALMANAC OF
ESSEX

Borley Church.

A Grim Almanac of

ESSEX

NEIL R. STOREY

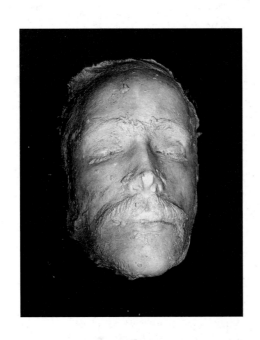

The
History
Press

The Grim Almanacs
are from an original idea by Neil R. Storey

This book is dedicated to all who have trod the beat in Essex.

Police officers and men at Southminster Police Station, *c.* 1902

Half title: Matthew Hopkins, Witchfinder-General
Title: Death mask of Frederick Guy Browne, the murderer of PC Gutteridge. *(Essex Police Museum)*

First published 2005 by Sutton Publishing
This edition published 2011 by

The History Press
The Mill, Brimscombe Port
Stroud, Gloucestershire, GL5 2QG
www.thehistorypress.co.uk

© Neil R. Storey, 2005, 2010

The right of Neil R. Storey to be identified as the Author
of this work has been asserted in accordance with the
Copyrights, Designs and Patents Act 1988.

British Library Cataloguing in Publication Data.
A catalogue record for this book is available from the British Library.

isbn 978 0 7524 6510 4

Typesetting and origination by The History Press
Printed in Great Britain

CONTENTS

Memorial gravestone to a Roman centurion of Camulodunum.

INTRODUCTION

Truth is always strange,
Stranger than fiction.
Lord Byron, *Don Juan* (1823)

Essex is a county with a long and fascinating past, but for the connoisseur of grim tales it soon becomes apparent that with so much history, so much life and so many people passing through or settling in the county over the years it is also endowed with a darker history through centuries of bloodshed, crime, dark deeds and witchcraft. Colchester can proudly claim to be one of the country's oldest continuously inhabited towns. Archaeological investigation has revealed a Bronze Age settlement on the site, while the Romans chose to found their first major English town, Camulodunum, here. Abundant evidence of their presence can still be seen in the ancient bricks and masonry incorporated in later buildings and churches in the town, and in the rich seam of archaeology that is revealed almost every time a building or factory site in the town is cleared. Here in the modern town it is easy to forget the bloodshed on the streets of the Roman town when Boudicca, Queen of the Iceni, and her force of thousands swept down to assault the garrison in the first century AD. Taking the city on the second day of battle, they slaughtered every man, woman and child in the town.

Every invader since the Romans has espied the navigable rivers and beaches of Essex and marked them as potential routes for raids or invasion. After the Romans came the Saxons and Danes, who fought violently for the territory in battles such as those at Maldon in 991 and Assandune (Ashingdon) in 1016, which have become the subject of epic poems and folklore. In 1348 the Black Death raged through Essex, scything down thousands in a harvest of death. A number of villages in the county suffered so many deaths they became depopulated and were abandoned. In 1381 it was an Essex priest named Jack Straw who led the county's rising in the Peasants' Revolt; marching on London, the men of Essex merged with Wat Tyler's Kentishmen and stormed the capital.

After the accession of Mary Tudor to the throne in 1553 the horrific purging of Protestants did not pass the county by. Seventy-two men and women were burnt at the stake for their faith in Essex, chiefly at Stratford, Brentwood and Colchester (where no fewer than twenty-two people were sent to the flames in just three years for their beliefs). In 1588 the peace of the county was shattered again with fears of a Spanish invasion. On 27 July the Armada reached Calais and a false alarm was spread that Spanish soldiers had landed and were marching on London. On hearing this, Queen Elizabeth went to her garrison at Tilbury and delivered her defiant speech, including the immortal lines, 'I know I have the body of a weak and feeble woman, but I have the heart and stomach of a king, and of a king of England too; and think foul scorn that any prince of Europe should dare to invade my realm.'

The summer Assizes of Essex in 1566 saw the first notable trial for witchcraft in England after such practices were outlawed in 1563. Three women, Elizabeth Francis, Agnes Waterhouse and her daughter Joan, all of Hatfield Peverel, stood charged with witchcraft. All the elements that were to become common features of the seventeenth-century witch persecution – such as selling of souls or pacts with the devil, animal familiars (in this case a cat called Satan or Sathan) rewarded or 'bought' with drops of blood from the witch, bewitchment of children, magical appearances and killing of animals, infliction of bodily afflictions and death by curse – were brought up at this

Dancing with the Devils.

The Devil presents a witch with a familiar.

trial. Agnes Waterhouse was the only one of the three accused to be executed, thus gaining the dubious honour of having been the first 'witch' to be subject to full judicial trial and execution in early modern Britain.

In 1582 came the infamous trial of the witches of St Osyth. Thirteen women stood accused, ten of them on charges of 'bewitching to death'. Six were found guilty and sentenced to death but only two actually went to the gallows: Elizabeth Bennett, who had confessed to killing a man and his wife by witchcraft, and Ursula Kemp, who was indicted for three deaths by bewitchment between October 1580 and February 1582. She eventually confessed and was found guilty on all three counts. In 1921 the skeleton of a woman was found in a garden in Mill Street, St Osyth. Careful excavation and examination revealed she had been 'pinned' to the ground with iron spikes through the joints – an ancient practice said to prevent a witch's spirit 'walking abroad and causing mischief'. The skeleton was believed to be that of Ursula Kemp, and coachloads of tourists came to gaze into the open grave.

In 1589 the third major trial of witches was staged at Chelmsford. One man and nine women were brought to trial, most of them on charges of bewitching persons and livestock to death or of spoiling livestock and goods. Joan Cony, Joan Upney and Joan Prentice were all found guilty and executed within two hours of sentencing, all of them 'confessing their crimes on the scaffold'. The active persecution of witches by judicial process in Essex then quietened down until the fears and uncertainties generated by the English Civil War manifested themselves in a number of witch scares where poor, elderly people, often widows, who made a few coins by offering charms and natural remedies, were accused of turning their supposed magical skills against their neighbours or those they disagreed with. The pressures exerted on society by the war exaggerated suspicions into certainties and led to a frenzy of witch-hunting. Ports and coastal areas are always more susceptible to new ideas from abroad so it is no surprise that the mass persecutions of witches' covens in Germany (which allegedly indulged in diabolical pacts, used familiars and regularly communed with the Devil himself) rubbed off on East Anglia.

One name comes to the fore at this time: Matthew Hopkins. A man with a spurious legal background, he was the keeper of the Thorn Inn in the dockside town of Mistley and no doubt heard every tale about witches on the continent. He was soon styling himself the 'Witchfinder-General' and claimed to have in his possession 'the Devil's list of all English witches'. Hopkins encouraged such methods as 'swimming' witches, and his small team of 'searchers' would prick the bodies of suspected witches to find 'the Devil's tit' – an area insensible to pain from which, he alleged, the witch's familiar would suckle her blood. Physical torture was officially not allowed but Hopkins was not deterred: severe sleep deprivation, forced walking until the feet blistered, solitary confinement and tying up those accused cross-legged for days on end were some of the methods he used to extract confessions of witchcraft. At one of the witchcraft trials manufactured by Hopkins in July 1645 he presented no fewer than thirty-two 'finds' at the County Sessions held at Chelmsford. Four of his 'finds', aged 80, 65, 60 and 40, had already died in prison before the Sessions opened. Hardly surprisingly, Hopkins and his team had extracted confessions from most of the 'finds'. Most of these confessions saw the accused admit to committing malevolent acts and keeping familiars like moles, a squirrel, a yellow cat and even a mouse named 'Prick-ears'. Twenty-eight were sentenced to be 'hanged by the neck until they be dead'. Nineteen of them were 'swung' right away, five were reprieved and the rest remanded to the next Sessions. Most of those who were left were still in gaol in March 1648.

Despite the efforts of the Witchfinder-General, a strong belief in witchcraft lingered on in the villages and hamlets of rural Essex. Throughout the nineteenth century and even into the early twentieth century it was common practice in the county to turn to local 'cunning folk', those well versed in cures, philtres and 'natural magic', to assist in medical matters, social problems and even matters of the heart. If you suffered with the likes of warts, had a cut that would not heal, wanted assistance in the birthing of a child or animal, desired an insurance for healthy livestock and good harvests or feared that a malevolent witch had cursed or overlooked you or a member of your family, then a quiet trip up the lane to the ramshackle cottage of an old cunning man or woman was the answer.

James 'Cunning' Murrell and George Pickingill of Canewdon were just two characters who stand out in more recent times. James Murrell, known to most as 'Cunning' Murrell, stood no more than 5ft tall but was arguably one of the most powerful witches ever seen in Essex. He was born in Rayleigh but settled

in Hadleigh, and it was said he could 'do anything, cure anything and know anything, past, present and future'. Locals said he possessed the evil eye and that once in a magical duel he summoned up all his powers and ordered his opponent to die – and die he did! George Pickingill, the last Witchmaster of Canewdon, took over the position when 'Cunning' Murrell died. Known to most locals as 'Old George', he came from a long line of Romany sorcerers; it was believed he had sold his soul to the Devil and had a parchment to prove it! If you dared creep up to his cottage at night it was said you might see 'Old George' dancing by the flickering flames of his fire, with his white mouse familiars and furniture joining in the dance with him! Local folklore tells that 'Old George' met his end in 1909 when he was thought to be about 100 years old. On a dull and windy day he was strolling by the churchyard wall when his hat was blown over among the gravestones. As he climbed over to retrieve it, the sun broke momentarily through the clouds, casting the shadow of a headstone in the shape of a cross over George's face. It killed him instantly.

Even in the nineteenth century witchcraft prosecutions were still being brought before local magistrates but were luckily treated with the contempt

The Colchester 'Mad Lizzies', thought by many, especially youngsters, to be witches.

such actions had long deserved. However, if the magistrates did not take action the locals sometimes took matters into their own hands which resulted in elderly or marginal folk being 'swum' in dirty local ponds and dykes; in one case in 1857 the rector of East Thorpe had to physically stand guard at the door of a supposed witch to prevent her suffering this treatment. In another case at Sible Hedingham in 1863 the man accused was swum – and died as a result.

Invaders, slaughter, warfare, plague, the burning of heretics and witchcraft are only a few of the grim offerings from Essex. I have found that once one scratches the surface of any county's history you soon come across darker tales, and Essex is no exception. In a county which produced William Calcraft, the country's longest-serving hangman, and can boast one of the earliest police forces, it is hardly surprising to find numerous accounts of public executions, murders, crimes and criminals. In this cornucopia of the macabre, these jostle for position with grim tales of dragons and mysterious beasts, visitations of the Devil, a flayed Dane, ghosts, freaks, strange deaths, disasters, horrific old punishments and repulsive prisons. This book has been made possible by generations of collectors, historians, authors and reporters who included strange stories and detailed accounts in their publications; I have simply noted them down and followed their lead, planning to do something one day with the file marked 'Strange Essex'. Having enjoyed generous and privileged access to police archives, coroners' reports, inquest accounts, assize records, private collections and public libraries, I have plumbed the depths of many of the grimmest long-forgotten records of the past. Join me on a journey along the darker paths of Essex's history – if you dare!

JANUARY

Governor and staff of Springfield Gaol, Chelmsford, 1905.

1 JANUARY **1961** Lorry driver Sidney Ambrose pulled his truck into a lay-by near the village of Ridgewell to answer a call of nature. Walking a few yards off the road he stumbled across the half-naked body of a young woman lying under a blackberry bush. Within twelve hours the body was identified as that of Jean Sylvia Constable (20) of Halstead, who had left home the previous day to go to a New Year's Eve party in London. She had been seen in a couple of Braintree pubs drinking with two men, David Salt (20) and USAAF Staff Sergeant Wills Eugene Boshears (29). Somewhat the worse for drink, all three went back to Boshears's flat at Great Dunmow. Salt and Jean Constable soon went into the bedroom while Boshears remained in the lounge, drinking. Later the couple reappeared, and continued drinking until they fell asleep in the lounge. Salt woke up at about 12.45am and woke Boshears to ask where the nearest taxi rank was. When he left, Salt believed Boshears and Constable were both asleep. At his trial for the girl's murder, Boshears claimed he only awoke when he 'felt something pulling at my mouth. I was not awake but this woke me up, and I found I had my hands around her throat. Jean was dead.' In panic Boshears disposed of the body in the lay-by where Ambrose found it. Despite the doubts expressed by the eminent pathologist Professor Francis Camps on the possibility of whether he could have carried out the strangling while he was asleep, the jury, after almost two hours' deliberation, found Boshears not guilty.

2 JANUARY **1943** William Henry Turner was a deserter from the army; playing on the goodwill of the British populace in wartime he deceived his way into people's homes purporting to be a corporal on leave who was unable to find accommodation. After he left, those who had shown him such generosity soon found he had forced the locks on wardrobes and drawers and stolen clothes and loose cash. On this day he received no response to his knock at the door of 19 Audley Road, Colchester. Assuming the house was empty he opened the door with a wire. Entering the house Turner discovered the occupant, 82-year-old Ann Wade, bending over a chair. Turner claimed he rushed up from behind and put his arm around her neck and she 'just went limp'. He carried her to another room. Suddenly there was a knock at the door, and a man asked for Ann Wade. Turner, giving nothing away by his demeanour, said she had gone out. Returning to the body Turner callously pushed it under a bed, then he stole some money and left. He was soon apprehended and put on trial for Wade's murder. Turner then changed his story, claiming he had been working in Ann's garden and had placed his arm around her neck while larking around. The first jury failed to agree on a verdict but at the second trial there was no hesitation and a guilty verdict was returned. Turner was executed on Wednesday 24 March 1943.

3 JANUARY **1873** Rettendon windmill mysteriously caught fire and was burnt down. As the hose of the horse-drawn pump fire engine extinguished the last of the flames a few locals breathed a sigh of relief, not only because the fire was out but also because they knew this event would put paid to what some believed was the curse of Rettendon mill. Over the last few hundred years a number of mills had stood on the site. One was erected in 1797 to replace its seventeenth-century counterpart, but it was said that the deal concerning the purchase of the old mill and the surrounding land had gone 'sour' and the aggrieved party had literally cursed the site. The first major tragedy occurred just a short time after the new mill began work: a little girl named Elizabeth Jeffries toddled into the path of the turning sails and was fatally wounded. In 1853 George Borrodell (24), the miller's son, tried to push a wheelbarrow through the gap in the sails as they turned. He was caught square on and died of his wounds five hours later. Peace then descended on the mill for the next twenty years until 3 January 1873, when the mill was found on fire.

1894 *In suspicious circumstances?* Police Sergeant John Harvey and his colleagues were making routine enquiries in the Ardleigh area. Harvey was seen by one of his constables at about 7.30pm, but he was never seen alive again. The following morning his body was discovered in a snow-covered well in the garden of one of the cottages. His watch had stopped at 8.21 and he had suffered injuries to his face, but exactly how they were caused was never proved with any certainty. He left behind a pregnant wife and three children. Exactly how his death came about remains a mystery.

4 JANUARY

Police Sergeant John Harvey. *(Essex Police Museum)*

1918 *Boy Racers.* Frank Chambers (17), Edward Tahon (17), Michael Flaherty (17) and William Beasley (age unrecorded) were remanded on a charge of stealing a motor cab and accessories, the property of Frank Love of Pancras Road, north-west London. Mr Love had left his cab in Museum Street; returning after about ten minutes he found it was missing. The following day he saw Chambers and Tahon on the street and asked if they knew anything about his cab. Amazingly they confessed they had stolen the cab and driven it hell for leather towards Southend – until the petrol ran out. They had then abandoned it at a side turning near Leigh Church. Essex police found the cab and the four boys involved were tracked down and arrested. During questioning, Flaherty said, 'We saw the cab and jumped into it. Chambers drove it away. I wish I could drive like Chambers.'

5 JANUARY

1873 The head and under gamekeepers were out watching for poachers on Sir Thomas Western's estate at Rivenhall when in the early hours of the morning, they spotted a band of six poachers armed with guns and sticks. Their leader was recognised as one of the estate grooms, Alexander 'Racer' Cowell. The gamekeepers leapt out and surprised the poachers who fought back fiercely, hitting out with their sticks to get away. One of the keepers

6 JANUARY

THE FIGHT

A nasty exchange between poachers and gamekeepers.

heard a voice say 'Shoot them!', and after receiving a severe blow to his head from a shotgun stock he heard another say 'Out with your knife and finish him.' Although blinded for a few seconds and bleeding profusely from his head wound, the head keeper ran off and the other keepers retired with him. They quickly called the police. The keepers were able to identify Cowell both by sight and by the sound of his voice, and he was arrested the following day at Braintree. Brought before the Spring Assizes at Chelmsford, Cowell was found guilty of poaching with violence and the judge declared that he would 'make an example of him' in his punishment. Cowell was sent down for five years' penal servitude.

1872 Constable John Street of Foxearth observed three men making off from a local farm with some sacks. Street grabbed the thief with the largest sack but was immediately set upon by the two accomplices. Street grimly held on to the sack until the men ran off, then he gave chase and captured one of the men. The sacks turned out to contain seventeen fowls that the men had stolen and killed. Constable Street was the first member of Essex Constabulary to be awarded the merit star and was ordered to display it on a new uniform jacket when the case came to court.

7 JANUARY

1918 Official acknowledgement was given by Essex Constabulary to the valuable work of the voluntary patrols, led by Mrs Cantill and Miss Newton, in policing the young girls who were coming to the area and 'loitering around army camps' in the Brentford and Romford area. Captain Unett, the Chief Constable, suggested the employment of six uniformed policewomen to be divided equally between Brentford, Romford and Grays. Thus Essex had its first WPCs – but only briefly, for they were all made redundant in October 1919. It was to be another twenty-five years before Essex welcomed women on to permanent placement within its ranks – the last county force in England to do so!

8 JANUARY

1683 It appears the medieval belief that the touch of a monarch could cure King's Evil (scrofula) was still alive and well in Essex in the late seventeenth century. Philip Peck, Minister of Romford, records his issue of certificates given according to the order made at Whitehall on 9 January 1683 concerning persons affected by the disease called the 'King's Evill' in order 'to their being touched by His Majesty to the end they may be healed'.

9 JANUARY

1908 Fire broke out at the Church of England School in Wickford. All the children were successfully evacuated as soon as the fire was discovered. A telegram was sent to summon the Chelmsford Fire Brigade but they refused to attend because in his haste the sender had not signed it and the fire brigade did not know who to send the bill for their expenses to! Firemen from Billericay did attend but despite their promptness the school was practically gutted by the time they arrived.

10 JANUARY

King Charles II.

11 JANUARY

'Jenny' Voller.

1899 Police investigations into 'The Barking Horror' continued. The body of 5½-year-old Mary Jane 'Jenny' Voller had been discovered in early January. She had been murdered and her body thrown into a narrow, muddy stretch of water known as Loxford Brook about 40 yards behind the shops on Harpour Road in Barking. The child had only been 'sent across the road' by her mother to buy a pennyworth of linseed. Fears were aroused when she failed to return. Her anxious parents went to the shop and found she had never arrived there, nor had she been seen in any other shops in the area. When her body was recovered it was found to be covered in scratches 'similar to those caused by scissors'. All that was missing were the few pennies she had in her pocket. Her murderer was never found.

12 JANUARY **1843** *The Times* published a comment on the proceedings of the last Quarter Sessions for the county of Essex, remarking that the report would doubtless be 'read with a strange mixture of wonder and disgust by all who take an interest in the important subject of prison discipline'. It went on to say that the prison was overcrowded, with living space in some of the cells limited to about 4ft by 6½ft per prisoner; there was no heating and little or no ventilation, and the inmates were said to be reduced to weakness and ill-health through insufficient diets and clothing. Scurvy was rife. The eventual outcome of such reports was the enlargement of the prison by 115 cells and a full review of procedures.

13 JANUARY **County Gaols and Bridewells of Essex visited by Prison Reformer John Howard**
The County Gaol at Chelmsford was visited by Howard and his representatives on no fewer than six occasions between 1774 and 1783. Unusually, some of the gaolers around this time were female. Susannah Taylor, for example, was followed by John Reynolds, who was succeeded by his widow. They received no salary but were granted fees for debtors and felons of 15s 4d each and were granted £1 5s for taking prisoners due for transportation from London to Gravesend if not more than seven in number (above seven they were paid the slightly lesser sum of £1 1s). They boosted their income by taking a 'garnish' from prisoners wealthy enough to pay for comforts like extra food, easing of restraints and straw for warmth. The sign in the tap room said it all: 'Prisoners pay Garnish or Run the Gauntlet.' The chaplain, the Revd Mr Morgan, was the highest-paid gaol official with a salary of £50, while the long-suffering surgeon Mr Griffinhoofte received a salary of £25 for attending both the prison and bridewell inmates. Howard was not impressed with the gaol: 'The old prison was close, and frequently infected with the

gaol-distemper. Inquiring in October 1775 for the head-turnkey, I was told he died of it.' When the new County Gaol at Chelmsford was visited by Howard in 1779 he was impressed, stating that it 'exceeds the old one in strength and convenience as much as in splendour. The county, to their honour, have spared no cost.' He recorded commodious rooms with vaulted ceilings for debtors and prisoners, courts, pumps and the segregation of sexes but he felt the cribs and cradles supplied for the babies of prisoners could be improved in standards of health and cleanliness and he noted there was no bath – a special concern as the prisoners in the cells were 'too much crowded at night'.

1862 Rebecca Law (24) hammered on her mother's door in the village of Langley in the early hours of the morning. Holding her 6-year-old son by the hand, she was in a very distressed state and covered in blood. She soon confessed to murdering her husband Samuel (27), a rat catcher by trade, and her 16-week-old baby Alfred. A police officer from Newport was summoned and soon the murder scene – the Laws' cottage at Starlings Green near Clavering – was uncovered. More than a hundred deep cuts and slashes had been made to Sam's face and neck, while the poor baby had been killed with a hammer. Rebecca Law was brought before the Lent Assizes. When questioned about the murder, she claimed, 'All the time I was hitting him there was a noise on the stairs. They kept blundering up the stairs – I mean the devils – but I wasn't afraid.' Testimony from medical authorities and the chaplain stated she was a 'melancholic' and a 'religiomaniac'. Found not culpable for her actions, she was removed to an asylum. **14 JANUARY**

1881 John Wilkinson (16) was brought before the Assizes at Chelmsford charged with the manslaughter of William Butler on Bridge Marsh Island near Latchington. On the evening of 5 December 1880 Mrs Marsh, who lived on Bridge Marsh Island, sent for her friend Charles Butler after she heard an intruder on her premises. Butler arrived with John Wilkinson and another lad named Rogers; they searched the house and immediate area but no intruder was found. Butler went home, leaving the boys as protection, after advising Mrs Moore to find and load her gun, if she had one. She duly brought the gun to Wilkinson who loaded it and fired it to make sure it worked. Then he loaded it again. Later that evening Rogers went outside saying he had heard someone, and Wilkinson followed with the loaded gun. They heard voices and both young men issued challenges but received no reply. They went a little further. Suddenly a man jumped out and seized Rogers violently by the throat; Rogers cried for help and Wilkinson fired at the assailant, felling him instantly. They brought a light and to their horror found it was Charles Butler's nephew William. He had been walking with his cousin Robert on the sea wall when he heard the boys' challenges; Robert had walked on but William probably leapt on Rogers as a prank. The judge asked the jury to consider if the gun was set off to frighten or injure the deceased; without a minute's deliberation the jury returned a verdict of not guilty and the prisoner was discharged. **15 JANUARY**

16 JANUARY **Old Punishments: the Scold's Bridle**

Alfred Hills MA was Clerk to the Justices of the North Hinckford and Halstead benches for twenty-two years between 1928 and 1950. A well-known and respected historian, he was a regular contributor to *Essex Review* for thirty years. Among his collection of bygones (which made up the foundation collection of Braintree Museum) was a scold's bridle (or branks), which he was so proud of he was even photographed wearing it! The bane of early modern British life was the scold – a nagging wife or a rumourmonger or malicious village gossip. The judiciary, with its usual robust approach to such social problems, devised the scold's bridle. There were several different designs but the basic construction consisted of a lockable iron framework in the form of a helmet-shaped cage that fitted tightly over the head. A small, flat, metal plate protruded into the unfortunate woman's mouth to hold her tongue down and prevent speech – hence the term 'hold your tongue!' Such devices were known to have been in use across the country until the late eighteenth century.

The scold's bridle.

17 JANUARY **1925** A woman's leg, complete with laced boot and stocking, was placed in the hands of Essex police at Ongar. It was discovered by Ongar motor-mechanic Mr W. Lane while he was travelling through Stanford Rivers on his motorbike at night. Feeling a bump under his wheels he got off to investigate and discovered the limb. A brief search of the area revealed no other body parts so Lane picked up the leg and took it to the police station. A contemporary newspaper report in *Weekly Dispatch* concluded, 'so far no one has come forward to claim it'.

18 JANUARY **1939** Pamela Coventry (9) left her home in South Romford to return for the afternoon lessons at her school on Benhurst Avenue. Her mother watched her walk up the road. Two of her friends were waiting for her on the corner of Benhurst Avenue but she never arrived. Pamela's body was discovered by chance by a cyclist who noticed 'a parcel' in a ditch by Wood Lane the next day. The post-mortem, carried out by the eminent pathologist Sir Bernard Spilsbury, revealed she had been strangled and sexually assaulted. Local man Leonard Richardson (28) was a prime suspect and was duly brought to trial,

but as each item of evidence which potentially linked him to the murder was dismissed and a clear alibi given and confirmed, the jury passed a note to the judge stating they did not wish to hear the summing up and declaring Richardson not guilty. The murder of young Pamela Coventry remains unsolved.

The ditch on Wood Lane where Pamela's body was found. *(Essex Police Museum)*

1927 Inspector Aroll and Superintendent Wood of the Railway Carriage Department were called to investigate the suspicious death of young Catford bride Mrs Dorothy Rose Rushton, whose body had been found on the railway near Wickford. She had planned to visit her brother but had not arrived and was reported missing to the authorities. Aroll and Wood found that if they opened the rear door of the train near the spot where she was found it slammed back with great force; there was no sign of a struggle, Mrs Rushton was not thought to be depressed and nobody reported anything suspicious on the train. There was one odd thing, though. A parcel sent to Brentwood police station from Southend was found to contain her handbag, inside which had been slipped the front page of the *Star* of 17 January, which featured an account of the woman's disappearance. There was nothing in the bag or on the parcel to show who had sent it. At the inquest an open verdict was recorded.

19 JANUARY

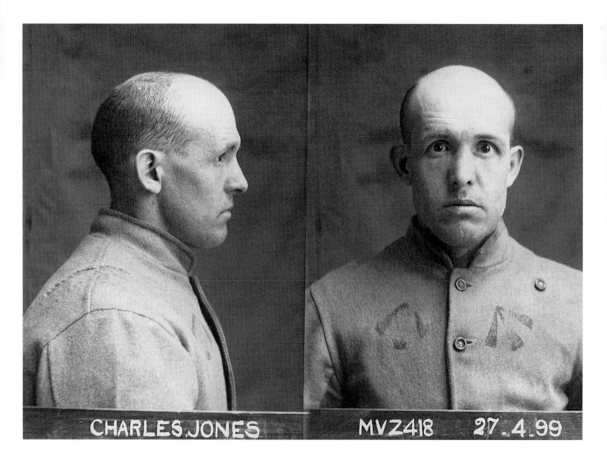

CHARLES JONES   MVZ418   27.4.99

20 JANUARY   **Old Punishments: Broad Arrow Men**
A familiar term for prisoners in the late nineteenth and early twentieth centuries was 'Broad Arrow Men', an epithet derived from the distinctive broad arrows or 'crow's foot' stamped on all prison uniforms. The origins of the symbol date back to the seventeenth century when a Master of Ordnance in the Tower of London began marking the weapons with an arrow-like device derived from his coat of arms to indicate they were Tower property. Over the years this symbol has been adopted by all government departments on various items of equipment – from military vehicle parts and rifles to rulers and paperweights – to denote Government Issue. The broad arrow was stamped onto prison garb not only to create a 'dress of shame' to be worn by convicts but also to make the clothes distinctive so they would be easy to recognise if they effected an escape. Broad arrows were discontinued on prison uniforms in 1922.

21 JANUARY   **1871**   George Kingsland, a prisoner in Springfield Gaol, was brought before Chelmsford magistrates. The previous day he was proceeding from the chapel to his cell when he threw himself off the corridor and fell 20ft to the basement below. The Chief Warder hurried to help him, but was astonished to find

Kingsland uninjured by his dive. Asked why he did it, he stated that he had murdered a man near Barnet four years previously and it was weighing on his mind. Repeating the story to other prison officials and the police superintendent, Kingsland claimed he had stabbed his victim in the throat for the few shillings in his pocket. It transpired that no crime of this nature could be traced, but Kingsland had previous convictions for vagrancy and his 'confession' was thought to be nothing more than a ruse to secure him further shelter in gaol during the winter months.

1810   The Revd Joseph Jefferson left Chelmsford in his carriage between 7.00pm and 8.00pm to go to London, with one servant, Joseph Sharpe, following the carriage on horseback. Halfway between Chelmsford and Ingatestone Sharpe passed a tall man carrying a trunk – which looked remarkably like one which belonged to his master. Sharpe thought little more of it. On their arrival at Ingatestone it was found that the straps had been cut through and both Jefferson's trunks had been robbed from the back of the carriage. A hue and cry was raised and a thorough search was made. Suspicion soon fell on two private soldiers, William Cooper and William Draper, from the New Barracks at Chelmsford. Some of the stolen property was seized in their barracks and the remainder found concealed in a ditch. Tried at the Assizes the following March on charges of grand larceny, their fate was sealed by Draper's partner Jane Evans. Fearing for her own neck for complicity in this crime, she testified that the men had brought the trunks to her hut in the barracks to divide their spoils. Both men were found guilty. Their ultimate fate is not recorded but the death sentence was usual for such a crime in 1810.

22 JANUARY

1847   Emma Davis, a Manuden servant-girl, had successfully concealed her pregnancy from her employers (because it could well mean dismissal) until this day when she had to abandon her chores and take to her bed. At 5.15pm two short cries were heard in her room. When a fellow servant looked in on her Emma claimed she had suffered a miscarriage and had disposed of the dead baby down the water closet. Upon investigation, the body of the baby was discovered at the bottom of the tank of effluvia, a tape wound tightly around its neck. Brought before the Assizes, Emma fainted as the surgeon described how the baby had died. Her sentence was very lenient for the crime – 18 months with hard labour.

23 JANUARY

Essex beliefs and omens that warn of the approach of the Angel of Death
If the church clock strikes the hour while the congregation is singing on Sunday there will be a death in the parish the next week.

24 JANUARY

If a grave is open on a Sunday, there will be another dug before the week is out.

During the interval between death and burial a body is spoken of as 'lying by the wall'. An old saying in the county states, 'If one lies by the wall on Sunday there will be another [corpse in the same parish] before the week is out.'

The ducking stool

Old Punishments: Cucking Stools and Ducking Stools

There is a good deal of confusion between these two punishments, because their names gradually blurred over the years until they have been assumed to mean the same thing. Both were widely used for the punishment of minor offences, especially in relation to strumpets and scolds. The cucking stool is far older and features in the Domesday Book; the miscreant was simply seated on it in a public place, often with a sign about their neck describing their offence. There is no evidence to suggest the cucking stool was used for submerging offenders in water. The ducking stool, in contrast, was a punishment to be dreaded. Probably introduced in the sixteenth century, it consisted of a chair or stool fixed to the end of a long pole. When the culprit, usually a scold or strumpet, was fixed in the chair the pole was lifted by human or mechanical contrivance and the chair's occupant ducked in water – usually a specially selected muddy or stinking pool near the village green.

1865 *The last public execution in Essex.* As the clocks of Chelmsford chimed 9 in the morning Ferdinand Edward Karl Köhl was executed. Despite the inclement weather, an immense crowd came to observe the spectacle. Köhl had been convicted of the murder of Christian Fuhrop on Plaistow Marsh, but he swore his innocence to the end. On the scaffold his last words were 'I am innocent, so help me God' – and then the drop fell.

27 JANUARY   **1934**   At about 1.00am a deadly exchange took place between shop-breakers and police officers on Hamlet Court Road, Westcliff. Edward Horsfall (25) and Roy McIlroy (23) broke into Bartlett's Drapers and stole 33s; Leslie Whyte (21), their getaway driver, was waiting outside in a taxi with the engine running. Beat officer PC Moses Abbott noticed the light of a torch inside the shop and the car outside, and asked Whyte about his reason for being there. Whyte said he had been telephoned by a customer and was waiting there for a pick-up. Abbott told Whyte to take him to Westcliff police station where he gathered reinforcements in the shape of fellow PCs Roper and Lawrence to investigate the possible break-in at Bartlett's. When they returned figures were seen moving in the shop. Realising the game was up, McIlroy smashed his way through a window at the rear and ran out of the passageway on to London Road, his face bleeding. As PC Lawrence closed on him, McIlroy fired a revolver at him. Luckily the bullet missed the officer, but the shot was fired at such close proximity it singed his knuckles! PC Roper quickly ran up and dealt McIlroy a blow on the head with his truncheon. Dazed, McIlroy then ran off up Ceylon Road with Lawrence and Roper in pursuit. The search for him ended when his body was found on a gravel pathway at the side of a house on Elderton Road. He had taken his own life with a single shot to his right forehead. Whyte and Horsfall were soon captured and stood trial at the London Sessions in February.

28 JANUARY   **Grim Tales of Essex**
Rayleigh Fair was held annually on Trinity Monday, and in its heyday in the eighteenth century it was truly infamous for the 'lowest kinds of entertainment for the sport of the lowest sorts'. Here among the shows and stalls moved cutpurses and dippers (pickpockets) a-plenty. One notorious competition staged there was to see who could swear the largest oaths and tell the biggest lies. Disputes and old animosities were saved up for the day and then settled in free fights for the delectation of the fair-goers, while those who had infringed parish laws were ordered to be excluded. Instead they had to do penance for the day, sitting in the parish church wrapped in a white sheet. No wonder this festivity gave rise to a once-popular term of derision –'as rough as Rayleigh Fair'.

An old dame of Essex.

29 JANUARY   **Essex Witches and Witchcraft**
In 1908 an old Essex village dame whom many of the villagers still turned to for folk remedies and assistance at birthing children and animals was accused of 'overlooking' a

local man. He believed the old woman had borne a grudge against him and brought him bad luck and prolonged sickness, which was apparently incurable by conventional medicine. When the man challenged the woman's equally ancient husband it erupted into an argument and the old man was assaulted. The case was brought before the magistrates but they were having nothing of this folklore and mischief and ordered the assailant to keep the peace. In the seventeenth century such accusations could well have seen the poor old woman brought before the witchfinder!

30 JANUARY

1649 The execution of King Charles I. Sir Henry Mildmay of Wanstead, one of the judges who condemned the king to death, was never allowed to forget this day. When Charles's son was restored to the throne retribution was swift. Many of those involved with the former king's death were immediately hanged or imprisoned, but Mildmay and two others kept their lives. Instead they were punished annually on the anniversary of the king's execution:

King Charles I.

they were drawn on a hurdle from Newgate to the gallows at Tyburn, where they could reflect on their lucky escape and the mercy of Charles II.

31 JANUARY

1911 *Execution of George Newton.* Newton (19) had been going out with Ada Roker for about three years and the pair had been engaged for six months. On the evening of 24 December 1910 Newton visited Ada at her parents' house in Stratford, London, but an argument flared up over a trivial matter. Newton would not calm down and Ada's family thought it best to leave the two of them to sort matters out alone. At about 7.00pm Newton left the house, pushing past Ada's sister on the stairs. She entered the kitchen and found Ada lying in a pool of blood on the kitchen floor. Her throat had been cut, her arms restrained by a strap buckled around her body just above the elbows. Newton

Essex police officers and men, Witham, 1892.

fled to the house he lodged in with his sister and her husband. He confessed all and was soon under arrest. At his trial Newton's defence claimed his mental state at the time of the attack was unsound, but the jury, convinced he had been responsible for his actions, passed the verdict of guilty of murder. Newton was executed at Springfield Gaol, Chelmsford, by John Ellis, assisted by William Conduit.

FEBRUARY

Bomb-damaged houses at Colchester after the first air raid
on the county, 21 February 1915.

1 FEBRUARY **1895** *The Big Freeze.* February 1895 was the coldest on record. Rivers froze solid and snow blew across the county. The body of Edmund Bishop (42) was found dead in the snow in Market Row, Saffron Walden, early in the morning of the 2nd; he had been missing all night. The inquest passed the verdict of 'death from exposure'. Later in the same month, on the 22nd, Elijah Sergeant (60) narrowly escaped a similar fate after collapsing on the side of the road shortly after leaving the workhouse.

2 FEBRUARY **1831** Reports were published of the recapture of escaped convict William Cooper (alias Waight) who had been at large since breaking out of Springfield Gaol on 30 September 1829. (He is thought to have been the first convict to escape from this gaol, which had only been fully completed at Michaelmas 1828.) Cooper had been incarcerated at the previous Midsummer Sessions for two years' hard labour for having passed a counterfeit shilling to Mrs Elizabeth Finch at Halstead. Posters bearing his description and offering a £10 reward for his apprehension were put up but no information was forthcoming until Cooper was recognised as an inmate of the Borough Gaol at Ipswich, Suffolk. This information was passed to George Wright, Keeper of the Halstead House of Correction, who communicated it to Mr Cawkwell, Governor of Moulsham Gaol. He knew Cooper of old. Ordered to convey two lunatic prisoners to Suffolk County Asylum, Cawkwell took his assistant Joseph Cracknell with him; having delivered their charges, they were taken to see the man in question. Charged with stealing silk handkerchiefs, this man had given his name as Newman of Chelmsford to the Ipswich authorities – but he was of course none other than William Cooper.

3 FEBRUARY **1895** Professor Ablett opened his course of lectures on phrenology at the General Baptist Chapel in Saffron Walden. The notion of phrenology – the 'scientific' means of ascertaining a person's character by the contours and bumps on his or her human head – was very popular in the nineteenth century. Particular consideration was given to the study of the 'criminal type'. Many of the most notorious murderers of the day had casts taken from their heads after execution for analysis by phrenologists.

4 FEBRUARY **1837** This day saw the death of eccentric clergyman the Revd George Somers Clarke DD (82), vicar of Great Waltham. Clarke had been confined to Moulsham Gaol on 22 May 1824 for contempt of ecclesiastical court. After his short sentence had been served in full, he insisted on remaining in the gaol, a request he was granted. His death was witnessed by Maria Wilson, a servant of the Cross Keys Inn, who had carried the parson's daily meals over from the pub for the last twelve years. When she entered his cell he was lying on the floor. She raised his head and spoke to him; he made no reply but only gasped twice and then expired in her arms.

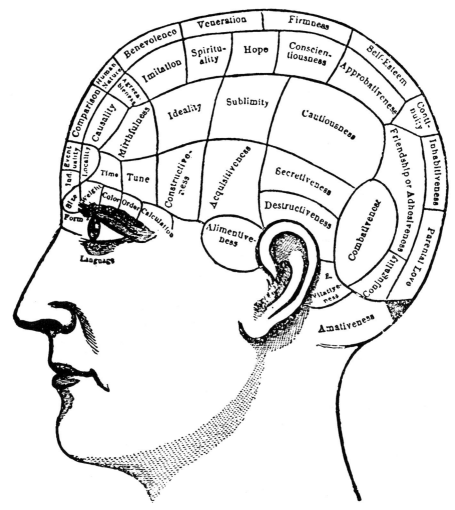

NUMBERING AND DEFINITION OF THE ORGANS.

1. AMATIVENESS, Love between the sexes.
A. CONJUGALITY, Matrimony—love of one.[etc.
2. PARENTAL LOVE Regard for offspring, pets,
3. FRIENDSHIP, Adhesiveness—sociability.
4. INHABITIVENESS, Love of home.
5. CONTINUITY, One thing at a time.
E. VITATIVENESS, Love of life.
6. COMBATIVENESS, Resistance—defence.
7. DESTRUCTIVENESS, Executiveness—force.
8. ALIMENTIVENESS, Appetite—hunger.
9. ACQUISITIVENESS, Accumulation.
10. SECRETIVENESS, Policy—management.
11. CAUTIOUSNESS Prudence—provision.
12. APPROBATIVENESS, Ambition—display.
13. SELF-ESTEEM, Self-respect—dignity.
14. FIRMNESS, Decision—perseverance.
15. CONSCIENTIOUSNESS, Justice, equity.
16. HOPE, Expectation—enterprise.
17. SPIRITUALITY, Intuition—faith—credulity.
18. VENERATION, Devotion—respect.
19. BENEVOLANCE, Kindness—goodness.

20. CONSTRUCTIVENESS, Mechanical ingenuity.
21. IDEALITY, Refinement—taste—purity.
B. SUBLIMITY, Love of grandeur—infinitude.
2?. IMITATION, Copying—patterning.
23. MIRTHFULNESS, Jocoseness—wit—fun.
24. INDIVIDUALITY, Observation.
25. FORM, Recollection of shape.
26. SIZE, Measuring by the eye.
27. WEIGHT, Balancing—climbing.
28. COLOR, Judgment of colors.
29. ORDER, Method—system—arrangement.
30. CALCULATION, Mental Arithmetic.
31. LOCALITY, Recollection of places.
32. EVENTUALITY, Memory of facts.
33. TIME, Cognizance of duration.
34. TUNE, Sense of harmony and melody.
35. LANGUAGE, Expression of ideas.
36. CASUALITY, Applying causes to effect.
37. COMPARISON, Inductive reasoning
C. HUMAN NATURE, Perception of motives.
D. AGREEABLENESS—Pleasantness—suavity.

5 FEBRUARY   **Old Punishments: The Birch**

Birching was a popular punishment for young petty offenders. Essex Police Force Orders from the early twentieth century read: 'Owing to the difference in age, nervous temperament and physical constitution, punishment must necessarily vary. The birching of children under 10 years should be less severe than in the case of older offenders. Birching to be administered by a Police Constable in the presence of an officer not below the rank of Inspector. Parents are to be invited to attend.'

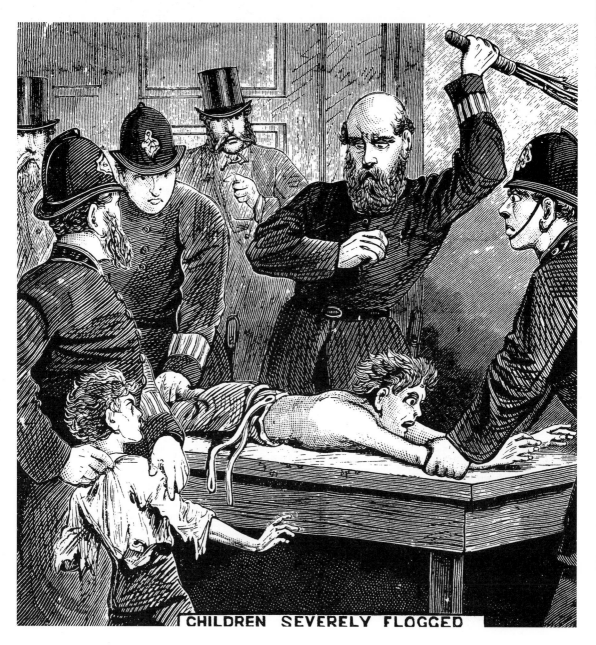

CHILDREN SEVERELY FLOGGED

ssex beliefs and omens that warn of the approach of the Angel of Death* **6 FEBRUARY**

A hare always comes and looks in at the stable door before the death of a member of the family.

The howling of a dog at night in front of your house, particularly near a room where there is a sickbed, betokens a death.

If the cuckoo gives his note from a dead tree it foretells the death of a relative.

The screech of an owl flying past the window of a sickroom signifies death is near.

7 FEBRUARY

1837 Appeals were published requesting information on the whereabouts of two convicts who had recently escaped from Springfield Gaol. The first to escape was James Monk; being 'diseased', he had been removed from his cell and taken to a segregation area used for vagrants suffering the same condition. At 1.00am on Thursday 2 February Monk broke away a slight window frame, forced himself between the bars and got out into the yard. From there he scaled the wall, let himself down 'and got clear off'. The other escapee was one James Cordrey, who had been detained on a charge of sheep stealing. In an effort to reduce escape attempts, at night prisoners were instructed to undress and leave their clothes in the passage opposite their cell doors. On Saturday 4 February Cordrey placed his hat on the floor and covered it with his smock-frock. To a casual observer it looked like a pile of clothes. Cordrey hid in the shadows while the cells were all locked up, then he slipped outside and escaped by climbing over the wall.

8 FEBRUARY

1886 Anthony Ben Rudge, James Baker and James 'Jack' Martin were executed at Carlisle for the murder of a policeman. PC Byrne stopped them at a checkpoint and questioned them about a burglary at Netherby House, Cumberland, the previous night. They had committed this offence and were doubtless alarmed to be apprehended so swiftly, and James Martin fired a gun at PC Byrne. Martin was also wanted for his part in the shooting of Inspector Simmons at Romford in 1885 (*see* 18 May). All three men were hanged by executioner James Berry, assisted by one 'Charles Maldon' – a man

Sir Claude Champion de Crespigny.

later revealed to be the colourful Essex baronet and magistrate Sir Claude Champion de Crespigny.

9 FEBRUARY   1895   Henry Johns, formerly of Cinder Hall, Saffron Walden, was found guilty of stealing £40 from his employer and was sent to prison for twelve months.

10 FEBRUARY   1941   A train from Norwich, labouring up the hill between Harold Wood and Brentwood, had come to a standstill when it was hit by the Southend-bound train. The rear carriage of the Norwich train was completely destroyed, wounding many passengers and leaving six dead.

11 FEBRUARY   1889   *The mystery of Samuel Mee.* A 47-year-old widower 'living in comfortable circumstances', Samuel Mee left his home in Birmingham on this day to spend a few days in London and the eastern counties. From London he travelled to Newmarket, where he wrote an unremarkable letter to his sister, and then he went to Bury St Edmunds and Manningtree, where he stayed in a hotel and saw an acquaintance. On the morning of the next day he took the train for London, leaving Manningtree a little after 9.00am. What happened next and why remains a mystery. He was in a carriage compartment with 'two respectable young persons', who subsequently testified that Mee had deliberately thrown open the carriage door with both hands and then jumped out while the train was passing Widford. He was picked up alive but severely injured and taken to a local infirmary, where he died the next day. The inquest decided he had 'died accidentally, not otherwise', but the Railway Accident Insurance Company refused to pay out on the claim. The matter was taken to court, where the jury, after due deliberation, found for the plaintiffs and ordered payment of £1,000.

12 FEBRUARY   **Grim Tales of Essex**

At Stondon Massey a mischievous spirit known as 'Jordan's Ghost' was considered to be responsible for a number of mysterious occurrences in the locality. They knew there was going to be trouble from the minute Jordan died in the early nineteenth century. It was said eleven clergymen assisted at his funeral, and when the sexton looked into the crypt he found the corpse lying outside the coffin. The coffin was later chained down – to keep bodysnatchers out and the

Jordan's tomb, foreground left, and Stondon Massey Church.

body within! The ghost of Jordan was soon seen wandering round the church-yard, and one story tells how a man tried to mow the spirit down with his scythe. The ghost raised its hand in defence, and when the body fell the hand stayed in the air!

1922 George Pearce (37) and his lady friend Alice Vincent (24) were enjoying a short break away at Southend. It was hoped the trip away would do George some good as he had been depressed after losing his job. They were staying at the Victoria Hotel, in separate rooms of course, but as they retired for the evening George asked for a kiss. Then suddenly he knocked Alice to the ground, sat astride her prostrate body and attempted to slash her throat with a razor. Alice fought back fiercely and screamed for help. The hotel proprietor soon burst in and pushed Pearce off Alice. Although badly cut about the face and minus an earlobe, she survived the attack. By the time the police arrived Pearce had realised the horror of his deed and had taken what was to prove a fatal dose of carbolic.

13 FEBRUARY

Southend beach.

1814 A proclamation issued on this day after a meeting of the magistrates of Dengie Hundred at the King's Head Inn, Maldon, read: 'It is resolved that immediate directions be issued to the Constables and other parish officers within the said hundred to be strict and vigilant in apprehending and bringing to Justice all persons who shall be found committing any offences against the Vagrancy Act. . . . All common beggars, gypsies and other persons wandering abroad and lodging in ale-houses, barns, out-houses or in the

14 FEBRUARY

open air, refusing or not being able to give a good account of themselves are considered Rogues and Vagabonds, and every constable or other person, who shall apprehend such offenders, are upon their conviction before a magistrate, entitled to a reward of 10s.'

15 FEBRUARY **1909** Margaret Mary Moult, better known to her convent sisterhood at the Abbey of St Mary, East Bergholt, as Dame Maurus, had joined the convent at 16 but had tired of the religious life and felt so trapped there that on this day she effected an escape. As evening fell she fled in pouring rain along dark country lanes towards Manningtree station, falling into several ditches along the way and only narrowly avoiding a pond. As she came within sight of the station, the bedraggled escapee in her muddied habit was found by

Margaret Mary Moult.

Sisters Philippa and Justina, who had been driven off in a trap in pursuit of the runaway. Maurus ran off again but was caught by the trap driver; to avoid being dragged back she clung grimly to a nearby fence. When she screamed porters from the station came running over. The driver's grip on her was relaxed and they all went to discuss the matter in the station. When Mr Swann the stationmaster intervened, the nun's pursuers left. He ordered refreshments and sat with Maurus by the fire in the waiting-room until the next train arrived and she returned to her family home in Camden Town, London. Her escape from the convent hit the headlines and 'seemed to be carried on every sandwich-board in London'. Ignoring letters imploring her to reconsider her actions, Dame Maurus reverted to her original name, and within two years, as Margaret Mary Moult, she had married Mr Page. She later penned her life-story, *The Escaped Nun*, which became a bestseller.

1897 John Denny was the respected foreman at the seed growers Carter, Dunnett & Co. at Lawford near Manningtree. Since Christmas 1896, however, Denny had been troubled. He confided to friends that his neighbours the Balls (Mr Balls worked for the same company as Denny as a shepherd) were 'scandalizing' him and his wife. By 13 February Denny had had enough. He confronted his neighbour. Mr Balls denied the allegations and challenged Denny to prove his charge. On the night of 16 February Mrs Balls heard a gunshot, and ran towards the front bedroom of their house. As she opened the door she heard another shot and was struck in the face by several pellets. She fell to the ground. Denny arrived at another neighbour's house soon afterwards, saying, 'I've shot someone at Balls's house; go see who it is, and lock me up.' Denny then panicked and fled. He was found on 18 February hidden in a heap of chaff covered with sacks by a policeman who was hunting for him with a dog. Brought before the Assizes in June, Denny was found guilty of unlawful wounding. After being warned that his sentence could easily have been much worse, he was sentenced to six months with hard labour.

1939 *Fire at Borley Rectory.* Borley, a sleepy village on the border between Suffolk and Essex, drew national attention in 1929 when poltergeist activity was reported at the rectory. When the Revd Lionel Algernon Foyster and his wife Marianne moved into the rectory in 1930 the activity greatly increased, with the words 'Marianne Get Help' being scrawled on the wall by invisible hands. Help was sought in the shape of Harry Price, the founder

The burnt-out shell of Borley Rectory, 1939.

of Britain's National Laboratory of Psychical Research. Following his work, Borley Rectory was proclaimed 'the most haunted house in England', amid much media hype. There has been considerable debate about the psychic phenomena Price found there, and some have even claimed to have helped him 'manufacture' the ghosts of Borley. None the less, as the fire raged through the rectory, some people apparently saw a young girl at the window. Even the village policeman had had the figure of a grey nun reported to him. Photographs of the ruins showed a brick in mid-air, and mysterious lights seen there during the war brought air-raid wardens running to enforce the blackout. In 1943 an excavation of the rectory site revealed a female skeleton complete with religious pendants. Nothing remains of the old rectory today.

18 FEBRUARY   1939   A man drove up to Colchester police station, introduced himself as George Butterworth (26) and informed the officer on duty that he had killed

his wife and her body was in the car outside. Wondering if it was just a sick joke or prank, the officer went outside – and found the body of Phyllis Butterworth (21) lying in the back of the car. Mr and Mrs Butterworth had been estranged for some time but George persisted in attempting to effect a reconciliation. He bought a Webley .22 pistol and some pellets, and hired a car to take his wife out for a trip to the countryside. They drove to Copford and had a fun day and evening out with friends. All seemed well until the journey home, when he stopped the car in a lane at Copford. The name of the 'other man' came up and an argument developed. Losing control, George beat Phyllis to death with the butt of the pistol. He pushed her body over onto the back seat and then drove to Colchester where he gave himself up at the police station. At his subsequent trial he was found guilty of manslaughter and sentenced to fifteen years' penal servitude.

19 FEBRUARY   1736   Rescue work continued after the massive storm on the 16th. Canvey and Foulness were both severely flooded: 'not a hoof was saved, and the inhabitants were taken from the upper part of their houses in boats'.

20 FEBRUARY   1961   Albert Henry Nickells (44), a charge-hand at Ford's in Dagenham, was brought before Essex Assizes. A devoted husband, he was devastated when his wife left him for another, younger, man. While paying her a visit, he stabbed her twelve times and then turned the knife on himself. Nickells suffered acute depression and had previously been in a mental hospital. Diagnosed as having a genuine mental dislocation and amnesia from the time of the offence, he was found guilty of manslaughter and sentenced to three years' imprisonment.

21 FEBRUARY   1915   *The first air raid on Essex.* A German aircraft crossed the sea-front at Clacton at about 8.00pm. Flying to Braintree, it dropped two incendiaries there and then returned to the coast via Coggeshall, Colchester and Shingle

Street, dropping high-explosive bombs on both Coggeshall and Colchester. At Coggeshall the bomb dropped in a field and caused a large crater, while the one dropped at Colchester fell in a back garden and demolished a corrugated iron shed. Luckily no lives were lost.

Bomb crater at Coggeshall after the first raid, 21 February 1915.

1917   The search for the killer of Louisa Burrow Walker (40) concluded after three days when Frederick Edward Livingstone (16) was arrested on London Road, Hadleigh. A witness had seen Miss Walker fall against a fence, stagger into the road and collapse dead near Tomlin's Corner; she had been shot in the back of the head. A young man was also noticed fleeing the scene. A description of him was circulated and the manhunt began. Once captured by PC Goby, Livingstone ignored the caution and confessed to murdering Miss Walker. The boy had been sent to St Albans to work on a farm but had run away, taking a revolver with him; he had killed Miss Walker because he was short of money. Found guilty of murder, Livingstone was sentenced to death but a petition for clemency was presented by Mr H.J. Mitchell of Hadleigh and Livingstone's sentence was commuted to penal servitude.

22 FEBRUARY

Grim Tales of Essex

23 FEBRUARY

The Court Book of Romford reveals some rough justice in the sixteenth century, a time when people really did fear for their mortal souls and believed in the fiery flames of Hell. John Bruce refused to bring a ring to his wedding ceremony, and refused to be married with one. Then he refused to appear before the court – and was officially excommunicated until he did!

24 FEBRUARY **1716** After being captured at the battle of Preston, James, 3rd (and last) Earl of Derwentwater, was executed on Tower Hill in London on this day for his part in the Jacobite uprising. In October 1874 his body was taken to the chapel at Thorndon Hall, Ingrave, and re-interred there. Dr Earle of Brentwood was present when the coffin was opened for identification, and his daughter recorded what he witnessed: 'The body was in three coffins. First an oak one. Then one covered with crimson velvet and then a leaden one. When the lid was raised they looked on the perfect face and figure of a young and very handsome man fully dressed with a lace cravat bound tightly round his neck. And even as they looked he was not, face and figure faded before their eyes and in its place a skeleton; the air had done its work, and they asked each other had they really seen this very man, dead for over 150 years.'

25 FEBRUARY County Gaols and Bridewells of Essex visited by Prison Reformer John Howard
Chelmsford Bridewell was visited on six occasions between 1774 and 1783. On the ground floor there were rooms for the sick, a large workroom and a kitchen. Prisoners were always kept within doors and the rooms were 'very offensive by the sewers'. Mr Ford, the keeper of the bridewell, had told Howard on one of his visits that he himself had been ill with gaol fever brought from the County Gaol. Ford was granted a salary of £30, while the under-keeper was paid £16; the garnish was 2s. There was an allowance of 3d per day per prisoner (or 3½d for sick prisoners), from which the inmates received 1½lb of bread, and a quart of small beer daily. The prisoners were employed in spinning wool at a penny a skein, with the county taking any profits.

26 FEBRUARY **Grim Tales of Essex**
James Wilson, 'the corpulent butcher of Romford', was a well-known character in the town during the late eighteenth century. He was best known for the peripatetic fashion in which he took his meals: it was not unknown for him to walk up and down the street while eating, a shoulder of mutton in one hand, a lump of salt in the bend of his arm, and a small loaf and a large knife in the other hand. It is recorded that on the last fast day before his death in 1799 he never quitted the church between morning and evening services, but repeated the Lord's Prayer and sang psalms in every pew in the church.

27 FEBRUARY **1885** Following the shooting of Inspector Simmons (*see* 18 May) Major W.H. Poyntz, the Chief Constable of Essex, wrote his report on the case. It included a considered suggestion for members of Essex Constabulary to be armed under the stringent rules by which revolvers were issued to police in outlying metropolitan areas: 'The revolver is to be carried in the holster on the belt on the right side and is not to be taken out of the holster for any purpose

Instructions issued to
Essex police officers
on the carrying of
revolvers. *(Essex
Police Museum)*

ESSEX CONSTABULARY.

The following regulations relating to the issue to and use by Police of Revolvers, having been approved by the Court of Quarter Sessions and Secretary of State, the Superintendents are to see that they are strictly adhered to :

1.—Revolvers are only to be issued to men who desire to have them when employed on night duty, and who can, in the opinion of the Divisional Officer, be trusted to use them with discretion.

2.—The Revolvers are to be kept at the stations to which men who are to use them are attached, the Officers in charge thereof being held responsible for their safe custody and efficient condition.

3.—A Revolver is to be issued to a Constable on parading for duty at a station on his own application only, at the time of parading. It is to be loaded by the Officer parading the relief, and placed in the holster. An entry is then to be made in the Occurrence Book, showing the number and name of the Constable to whom a Revolver has been issued and also the number of the Revolver.

4.—The Revolver is to be carried in the holster on the belt on the right side and is not to be taken out of the holster for any purpose whatsoever, except for self defence.

5.—Officers carrying Revolvers are to be strictly enjoined that they are only to be used in self defence where there is necessity for resorting to their use, as when the Constable is attacked by a person with firearms or other deadly weapon and cannot otherwise reasonably protect himself, a Constable (as a private person also) may resort to a Revolver as a means of defence.

6.—On going off duty, an officer to whom a Revolver has been issued at a station is to at once extract the cartridges, and hand it over next morning as early as possible to the Superintendent or Inspector in charge, who will, in the Officer's presence, carefully examine both weapon and cartridges, making an entry in the Occurrence Book of the condition in which they are delivered to him.

7.—The Officer having the use of a Revolver is to report on going off duty, every instance in which he has had occasion to remove it from the holster during his tour of duty, whether it has been used or not ; such reports are to be dealt with as "urgent" and submitted at once to the Chief Constable through Superintendents.

8.—Before a Revolver is issued to an Officer, he is to be properly instructed in its use, and a report of his competency submitted, through the Superintendent, to the Chief Constable, for his approval.

9.—A box will be supplied to each Station, and to each Officer, to whom a Revolver has been issued, in which it and the cartridges are to be kept locked up and the key retained always on the Officer's person.

10.—An Officer to whom a revolver is issued at an out detachment, and who is unable to parade at a station owing to distance therefrom, is to keep the box in a safe place locked up, and is invariably to extract the cartridges on returning from duty.

11.—Superintendents and Inspectors, when visiting their men's residences, are invariably to inspect and examine the box, revolver, and cartridges, to see that the weapon is in good order, and the proper number of cartridges accounted for.

CHIEF CONSTABLE'S OFFICE,
 CHELMSFORD,
  1st June, 1885.

W. H. POYNTZ,
 CHIEF CONSTABLE.

whatsoever, except for self-defence.' The County Justices accepted Poyntz's proposal and the first order for twenty revolvers was placed with Webley & Sons in June 1885.

28 FEBRUARY **1849** At about 1.00am Nehemiah Perry was disturbed from his slumbers by somebody entering the ground floor of his home, Strethall Hall. Knowing that his brother had retired to bed at the same time as him and that their housekeeper had gone home, Perry feared the worst. He had been on his guard since his acrimonious divorce from his gypsy wife, fearing reprisals from her family. Perry woke his brother, and the two men armed themselves and lay in wait for the intruder at the top of the stairs. Out of the darkness a figure emerged, wearing a sacking mask. By the sounds of it he was not alone. In an instant the masked man saw the Perry brothers and called to his companions to bring pistols. At this, Nehemiah replied with a blast from his shotgun. Not daring to go downstairs until daylight, the Perry brothers cautiously edged downstairs at dawn but the only person they found was their intruder, quite dead, shot through the breastbone. They removed his mask but they did not recognise the man. The villagers soon heard of the night's events and came to view the body, but nobody could name the dead man. A death mask was taken and circulated to neighbouring forces. Benjamin Taylor, the Chief Constable from Peterborough, managed to make an identification, assisted by the 'distinguishing features' recorded in gaol books. The dead man was Abraham Green (alias Woods), an East Anglian ne'er-do-well, who was known to many in the underworld as 'Little Abel'. Once identified, his body was packed into a game basket and sent to surgeon George Paget of Cambridge for dissection. It was accompanied by a note that read simply: 'Dear Paget, I have shot a burglar. [Signed] N. Perry.'

29 FEBRUARY **Grim Tales of Essex**
In 1816 an extraordinary character was recorded at Havering. Mrs Elizabeth Balls was a widow 'of about 60 years' and quite well off with an income of around £150 a year. She had a reputation for breeding outstanding livestock that commanded great prices at local markets. They were also, without doubt, the most privileged and spoilt animals in the county because she kept the animals in her house and considered them to be her family. She was known to have had up to fifty goats. In September 1815 it was recorded that her 'family' consisted of 14 goats, 2 sheep, 17 fowls and a French dog. No one was ever admitted to her dwelling except twice a year when a person was allowed to clean it since the building was 'nearly choked up with the accumulation of dirt from these creatures'.

MARCH

Colchester characters Grimes and Emma stop from their 'toils on the tramp' for refreshment, *c.* 1905.

1 MARCH   **1962**   Percy Alfred Blanks (46), an agricultural contractor, appeared at Essex Assizes accused of shooting dead Reginald Blackshaw. When asked about the shooting Blanks confessed, 'I shot him. He said I was lazy', and seemed more concerned about his overdue income tax papers. Although a hard worker, Blanks was described as 'always being in a muddle' and had difficulty costing his work, being reduced to guessing what he could charge. When assessed in Brixton Prison, his IQ was recorded as 75. He was found guilty of manslaughter, but in less than a week was ordered to be detained in a mental hospital for an unlimited duration.

2 MARCH   **1907**   On this Saturday morning a twelve-carriage passenger train bound for London collided with a goods wagon which had been left on the Up line at Chelmsford. The train driver had spotted it just in time and was able to reduce the speed of the impact. The truck was thrown off the rails but only minor damage was caused to his train. So grateful were the passengers for their lucky escape that many got out of their carriages to shake hands with the train driver, who, it is said, knelt at the trackside and gave thanks to the Almighty for their narrow escape from disaster.

3 MARCH   **1801**   The Chelmsford Assizes calendar for the forthcoming sessions was published and circulated on this day. A total of 118 prisoners were to stand trial. One of the twenty-eight persons sentenced to death at the Assizes was Robert Jewell, who was convicted for burglary. He begged to address the court, and was permitted. He stated he had been 'decently educated' and until the age of 35 lived a virtuous and sober life, 'until he had the misfortune of becoming acquainted with persons who were admirers of Paine's writings'. (Thomas Paine was a radical political writer who published *The Rights of Man* in 1791, supporting both the French Revolution and the overthrow of the British monarchy.) He had the writings 'placed in his hands' and became 'a convert to Paine's doctrines, and considered the Scriptures as cunning fables'. He concluded that he now saw the error of his ways, trusted in God and 'begged most earnestly that his children might be taken care of'. He was then taken to the cells to await his fate.

4 MARCH   **1856**   James Thurgood (29), his brothers Thomas (23) and William (22), and James Guiver (30), all labourers and 'athletic young men', were brought before the Assizes on the charge of wilfully murdering gamekeeper William Hales. The last three fellows breathed a sigh of relief when it was announced that the grand jury had dropped the capital charge against them; the case was to be confined to James Thurgood. As the evidence was given, it emerged that William Thurgood had suggested a night's poaching in Sir John Tyrrell's wood. They walked across the fields to Boreham and Duke's Wood, each man with a gun, hoping to bag a few pheasants. Joseph Wesby, his father James and William Hales were gamekeepers employed to protect the woods; hearing the shots they set off to try to catch the miscreants. Hales went in a slightly different direction and was soon heard calling, 'Come on mates, here they are!'

Joseph Wesby was closest to Hales when he heard a shotgun go off and saw Hales fall to the ground. The poachers then took to their heels. The Wesbys managed to catch hold of James Thurgood and took him back to Duke's Head Farm; once he was secured there they returned to the wood. When they found Hales's body his clothes were still smouldering. At the inquest Mr Copeland the surgeon agreed that Hales had not stood a chance with a shotgun fired that close to him. However, at Thurgood's trial it could not be proved beyond reasonable doubt who had actually fired the fatal shot. Nevertheless he was found guilty of being an accessory to the murder and was sentenced to death. Thurgood was not the least dismayed and replied in an impudent tone, 'Thank you sir; God bless you all!' His sentence was later commuted to imprisonment. All four also faced charges of night poaching. They pleaded guilty, and were given four years' penal servitude each.

Essex beliefs and omens that warn of the approach of the Angel of Death

Tablecloths and other linen, particularly sheets, were carefully examined for oval creases known as 'coffin folds' that signified imminent illness or a fatality in the household.

If a clock 'loses a stroke' or refuses to go properly, a death will be known to the family.

Three raps on a bed's head is an unwelcome greeting as it warns of death.

1867 Elizabeth Dann (23), a domestic servant and 'imperfectly educated', was brought before the Spring Assizes charged with the wilful murder of her illegitimate child. The court was lenient; as the judge pointed out, there was no direct evidence of foul play. Since she had concealed the birth of her child, only she would have known if the child was born alive or dead. To give her time for reflection and instruction in religion, and above all to set her up as 'a warning to those who indulge in vice', she was sentenced to eighteen months' imprisonment with hard labour.

7 MARCH   **1820** Thomas Cole was indicted at Essex Assizes, Chelmsford, for 'uttering' a forged Bank of England note. He admitted only to the lesser charge of possession and luckily for him no evidence was presented on the capital charge. His life was saved but he was sentenced to fourteen years' transportation.

8 MARCH   **Old Punishments: Oakum Picking**

Oakum picking was a common occupation for prisoners during the nineteenth century. The process could be carried out either in solitary confinement cells or with other prisoners (in silence) in workrooms or oakum sheds. Each prisoner was given a weighed amount of old ship's rope cut into lengths, often black with tar and deeply engrained with salt. Each piece of rope was unravelled into strands by rolling it back and forth on the knee with the palm of the hand until the meshes loosened; each strand was then separated and cleaned of the salt and tar on it. This 'stuff' was then used for caulking the seams in the sides and decks of wooden ships. Men, women and children prisoners all picked oakum; it was very hard on the fingers and rope cuts were common, as were blisters which proved very painful until the skin on the hands hardened to the work. Prisoners were expected to produce 3–4lb every two hours, and shifts of oakum picking could last up to twelve hours. At Tothill Fields Prison in London the boys (all under 17) could earn up to 17s a year for their oakum picking – literally money for old rope!

9 MARCH   **1871** John Pimlett Brearley, a publican of about thirty years, was brought before the Assizes accused of wounding with intent to inflict grievous harm on Captain John Bardoe Elliott. The facts of the case were that Elliott had had a relationship in the early 1860s with a young woman, but he had terminated this after his marriage to another. Elliott gave the first young woman an allowance, but in October 1866 she released him from all demands and began a relationship with Brearley. Brearly claimed his previous marriage was invalid and he and the young lady began to live together as man and wife. Discovering she had £300 deposited with a relative, Brearley sued for it as her 'husband' and finally received the money. He spent it frivolously, and plotted to obtain more by, in effect, blackmailing Captain Elliott. This worked for a while until Elliott finally refused to pay, so Elliott's former mistress then told his new wife all about her relationship with the captain. Elliott refused to have anything more to do with her. Next Brearley got hold of the love-letters the pair had exchanged long before, which were undated; pretending they were recent, he set them up as provocation. Obtaining a revolver and a thick stick, he angrily sought out Elliott. When the two men met, Brearley dealt Elliott a heavy blow to the head with the stick, which cut through to the skull. A fight ensued and Brearley drew his revolver. Bleeding profusely from his head wound, Elliott dodged around and seized the pistol by the barrel. As the men wrestled for control of the weapon, a shot was discharged, the bullet glancing off Elliott (actually striking off a button), but he was uninjured and he took his chance

to overpower Brearley and summon assistance. Brought before the Spring Assizes, Brearly refused counsel and defended himself, greatly prolonging the proceedings. Found guilty of unlawful wounding, he was sentenced to five years' penal servitude.

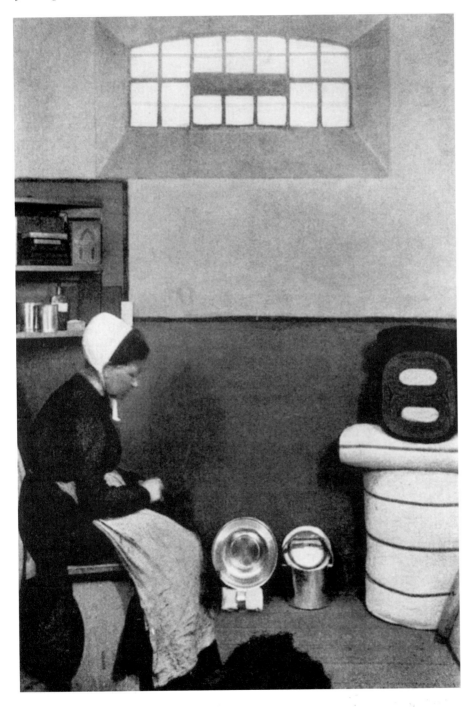

A female prisoner picking oakum.

10 MARCH **1800** At Essex Assizes Henry Hunsden (11) was found guilty of stealing various banknotes out of the letters from the post office at Chelmsford and sentenced to death. Upon hearing the dreaded sentence 'the little convict fainted away, and was supported in the gaoler's arms while sentence was passing upon him'. In the belief that the boy might yet receive royal mercy, the judge, Baron Hotham, gave the boy a respite, 'in order that due consideration may be had in what way mercy can be extended to him'.

11 MARCH **1891** Arthur Leatherdale (18) was indicted at the Assizes for the murder of his uncle Joseph Leatherdale at Salcot on 20 December 1890. Arthur lived alone with his uncle and helped in his business as a farmer and carrier. On that fateful day the old man was last seen at 8.40am. At 10.00am Arthur drove a party of seven to Colchester, and while there he was seen to spend more money than was his usual habit. That night and for the next three days Arthur stayed with one of his neighbours, having explained that his uncle was going away for Christmas. Arthur then went to stay with his uncle's married daughter, where he repeated the same tale about his uncle. It just did not ring true, so she telegraphed Joseph's brothers, with whom he was supposedly staying, and was alarmed to discover he had not arrived. She contacted the police and a search of Joseph's home was undertaken by a constable accompanied by two neighbours and Arthur. They found his body in a cupboard under the stairs. His head had been wrapped in a sack, and a large gunshot wound was found at the back of his head. A brick in the parlour floor, under which the deceased was known to keep his money, was lifted and all the money was found to be gone. Arthur Leatherdale was arrested and searched, and a number of caps and shot of the type that had killed his uncle were found on him. He declared: 'I was here when he was shot, with four or five others. I helped to put him in the cupboard. I shan't split; I'll take it all on myself.' At his trial it emerged that he came from a family with a history of insanity; his father was known as 'Crazy Charlie' and at least two of his relatives had died mad. The jury found him guilty and he was sentenced to death, but this was later commuted to incarceration.

12 MARCH **1821** Robert Gouldstone was indicted at the Lent Assizes held at Chelmsford for 'feloniously and maliciously' wounding a boar, the property of Robert Crush in the parish of Butsbury. The boar had strayed onto Gouldstone's land and caused considerable damage to his vegetables, and in a fit of rage he set about beating the beast with a large cudgel. The justice directed the jury that Gouldstone had not directed the attack against the owner of the pig, and a verdict of not guilty was returned; the justice did, however, chastise Gouldstone for his violence against the animal. Thomas Ayling appeared at the same Assizes charged with sheep stealing; found guilty, he was sentenced to death.

13 MARCH **1802** Highwaymen Edward Newman and David Wright were awaiting their fate in the condemned cells at Chelmsford. Both Irishmen, they had been

employed on the potato grounds near Stratford. Seeking enhancement to their meagre wages, they waylaid John Bennett, innkeeper of the Three Rabbits on Ilford Road, and robbed him on the king's highway. Unfortunately they were observed in the act by a mounted watch patrol. After an exchange of pistol shots both men were secured. Found guilty of the crime at the Spring Assizes, they were sentenced to death.

'Stand and Deliver!'

1821 Charles Linguard, William Hambleton and William Sans were brought before the Essex Lent Assizes for breaking and entering the house of Elizabeth Smith, a widow, at Springfield and stealing a considerable amount of silver plate and valuables. The men had been seen with bundles in their hands some 3 miles from Springfield in a lane which led to Billericay. When the alarm was raised a search was made in the lane for the bundles they had been carrying. An examination of two dunghills revealed some of the stolen articles: a dark lantern, a pair of pistols, a pig killer's knife, a pick-lock key, gimlets, a crowbar and other burglar's tools. Hambleton and Sans were soon traced and arrested at a Billericay pub. Linguard returned to the dungheaps but surrendered after a fierce chase. Stolen property and burglar's tools were found about his person. The evidence against all three was damning and after the guilty verdict was delivered the judge warned the prisoners 'not to entertain the slightest hope of mercy' before he sentenced them all to death.

14 MARCH

1817 Joseph Burrels and James Knight were convicted at Essex Assizes of stealing 8 bushels of oysters from an oyster-bed in the River Crouch, the property of the Burnham Oyster Company. They were sentenced to two and seven years' transportation respectively.

15 MARCH

16 MARCH **1875** On this day Mr *C.C.* Lewis, the coroner for South Essex, concluded the inquest on the body of Edward Ives (43), a convict at Springfield Gaol. Ives, a former soldier in the Royal Artillery, had been sentenced to ten years' penal servitude for the attempted murder of Sergeant-Major Leeson with a sword bayonet while at the Shoeburyness School of Gunnery. On the morning of Ives's death the warders were just opening his cell door when he rushed out and jumped over the balustrade, falling several feet onto the asphalt below. He died shortly afterwards from a fractured skull. At the inquest the deceased's sister testified he had served in India for several years, the implication being that the 'heat turned him'; apparently his father had also attempted suicide on no fewer than twelve occasions. The jury passed the kindest verdict; that of death while in a state of temporary insanity.

17 MARCH **1912** Captain Lawrence Oates was a member of the expedition led by Captain Robert Falcon Scott to reach the South Pole. Just 27 miles short of the pole they found the tracks of the Amundsen expedition and realised that they had been beaten to their objective. They struggled on and eventually reached the pole but it was on this day, Oates's birthday, during their journey back to base camp, that the brave captain, badly frostbitten and severely ill, realised he was holding back the progress of the expedition. He walked purposefully out of the tent into a blizzard, saying the immortal words: 'I am just going outside, I may be some time.' He was never seen again. Oates was a son of Essex and grew up at Gestingthorpe Hall (then known as Over Hall). He and his selfless bravery will never be forgotten.

18 MARCH **1810** Reports circulated on this day of the latest cases at the Assizes. John Houghton, described as 'a boy under fourteen', was a tap and post boy in the employ of Mr Chinnery at Abridge. The boy had left his employer with such haste that Mr Chinnery was alarmed enough to check his savings box; when it was opened it was found to be empty. Mr Chinnery applied to the constable for assistance and the lad was soon traced to his mother's house. Charged with the robbery, he freely confessed the fact but blamed another servant for instigating it. The jury had no mercy for this lad; he was found guilty and sentenced to death.

19 MARCH **1804** This day saw the execution of the only woman to be hanged at Moulsham Gaol, Chelmsford. Elizabeth Langham, the wife of a trooper in the 18th Light Dragoons stationed at Colchester, had been found guilty of the murder of her infant child. Physically and mentally wrecked by the experience of prison, her crime and the dreadful sentence passed on her, she had to be assisted onto the scaffold. In front of a large crowd 'unusually quietened' by the spectacle, she suffered the ultimate penalty of the law.

Moulsham Gaol,
c. 1804.

1810   *The Peacekeeping Highwayman.* Mesrach Reed began his confinement   20 MARCH
in the House of Correction on this day, having escaped a far worse fate.
A private in the King's Dragoons, Reed had been convicted of feloniously
stopping a man 'on the king's highway' at Easty Ford, and attempting to rob
him by aiming a pistol at the man's head. Reed was traced to his barracks
near Romford within the hour and put into gaol to await trial. He was
found guilty and would have been sentenced to seven years' transportation
(perhaps even death) but through his 'active exertions during his
confinement in subduing a riot in the gaol' his punishment was reduced to
one year in the House of Correction.

1805   Accounts began to circulate across the county of the 'Trial of the   21 MARCH
Volunteers' at the recent Essex Assizes. A special jury was sworn in and
before them were brought Mr Wrenn, 'a gentleman of fortune', Mr Asplin,
'a doctor of physic, magistrate and Commander of the Volunteer Corps',
Mr Marshall Turner, a farmer, and Messrs Sumner, Kennet and Asplin. One
of these three was also a clergyman and magistrate. The prosecution was
brought by Mr Higgs, an innkeeper of Rayleigh. He claimed that a meal had
been ordered for twelve or fourteen people but only seven came to it, and they
drank steadily until 10.00pm, when they called for the bill. The guests judged
it extortionate and instructed the innkeeper to knock off 1 guinea. Higgs
refused. The defendants then shut the door and set about Higgs, beating him
and dragging him about the floor. His cries brought neighbours and peace

officers, who promptly took some of the defendants into custody. However, they were persuaded by one of the Volunteer officers to set them free again so the honour of the Corps would not be besmirched. The judge left it to the jury to say what recompense Higgs the innkeeper should receive, and he was awarded a total of 300 guineas.

22 MARCH **1806** *The last duel in Essex?* John Fisher and Henry Torrence were officers in the 6th Regiment of Foot. It was alleged that Torrence had insulted Lieutenant Fisher while on parade by striking him and calling him a coward. Despite the efforts of his brother officers, Torrence would not calm down and apologise but instead sent for his pistols. The duel was formally convened on Galleywood Common with Seconds and an assistant-surgeon present. Shots were exchanged and Torrence fell, shot in the groin. Fisher and the Seconds Guy Campbell and John Blakeman were brought before the court in the July Assizes on the charge of murdering Torrence but no witness would give direct evidence that the duel actually took place. The regimental Assistant-Surgeon, Constantine John Day, made a typically unhelpful statement: 'My Lord, whoever were the unfortunate parties in the affair, I am myself so deeply implicated that I cannot give evidence consistently with my own safety.' The Lord Chief Baron said 'there was no evidence whatever against the prisoners' and accordingly they were acquitted!

23 MARCH **1818** George Lawford was indicted at Chelmsford Assizes for stealing a paroquet (sic), the property of Stephen Kempshead, an innkeeper of Chadwell. Lawford was caught with the bird after attempting to sell it on. Identification of the paroquet in question was proved in the court, where, to the great amusement of all, it was persuaded to repeat the phrases it was known to say, such as 'Waiter, bring a bottle of old port', 'Pipe all hands a-hoy!' and several other 'ludicrous exclamations'. Lawford was found guilty and sentenced to two months' imprisonment.

24 MARCH **Grim Tales of Essex**
In the parish of Tolleshunt Knights there was for generations an uncultivated spot of land. Legend tells that once it was proposed that a great house should be built on the site – but what the workmen erected by day the Devil came and knocked down by night. A knight accompanied by two good strong dogs was charged with watching the site at night for the destructive intruder, and sure enough Old Nick himself appeared. A struggle ensued and the Devil picked up a great beam and hurled it up a nearby hill, exclaiming 'Wheresoe'er this beam shall fall, there shall stand Barn Hall.' And so Barn Hall was built there. The Devil was, however, not done with the knight: he was so outraged at being interfered with he said he would have the knight's soul whether he was buried in the church or out of it! But the knight foiled the Devil by being buried half inside and half outside the church. The beam, however, was said to remain in the cellar of Barn Hall, cursed so 'no one can cut it without wounding themselves'.

1851 Sarah Chesham and Thomas Drory were executed at Chelmsford Prison on this day. Sarah was known as a dissolute woman in the village of Clavering, where she lived in wretched poverty with her farm labourer husband and her large family of children. During the winter of 1846/7 her youngest sons both developed mystery illnesses which eventually led to chronic stomach pains and death. Post-mortems revealed arsenic in their stomachs and Sarah was arrested for their murder, but at her trial it could not be proved that she had actually administered poison to them and she was acquitted. In May 1850 Sarah's husband developed an illness similar to that of their sons, and subsequently died. The earlier case had not been forgotten. Sarah was arrested and brought to court. All the evidence and the witness statements were damning this time, and having been found guilty she was sentenced to death. She was joined on the scaffold by Thomas Drory, who had been found guilty of strangling his pregnant mistress. The high profile of the Chesham case and the 'event' of a double execution brought a crowd of 10,000 people, mostly women and farm labourers, to the scene. Chesham and Drory both took several minutes to die, struggling for breath on executioner Calcraft's short ropes. After hanging for an hour the bodies were cut down; Drory was buried in the prison precincts but, owing to a technicality of her conviction, the body of Sarah Chesham was released to her family. Her son took the body in its coffin by cart to Clavering, where she was later buried without ceremony.

25 MARCH

1555 *Protestant Martyr.* William Hunter, a 19-year-old apprentice, was caught reading a Bible by one Atwell, a servant of Bishop Bonner. Taken to Bishop Bonner, he was offered £40 to set up his own business and the chance to become a Freeman of London if he would recant from 'meddling with scriptures'. Young William replied courageously, 'I cannot find in my heart to turn from God for the love of the world.' After his trial he was sentenced to be burnt on this day at Brentwood. Offered pardon again on the morning of his execution, William would not recant and was chained to the stake as the faggots were piled around him. As the flames leapt around him, he exclaimed 'I am not afraid, Lord!' and prayed 'Son of God shine upon me.' It is said that the sun then broke through the clouds and shone full on his face until the flames consumed him.

26 MARCH

1829 James Cook (16), a young cow-boy on the farm of William Green of Witham, was found guilty of starting a fire which damaged his master's buildings and stacks. Such a crime still carried the death penalty, and despite pleas for leniency the sentence was carried out to the letter. James Cook was executed above the gateway of Springfield Gaol for arson. His execution drew a massive crowd and many women were recorded as 'openly weeping'.

27 MARCH

1752 This day saw the execution of lovers Elizabeth Jeffries and John Swan for the murder of Joseph Jeffries, Elizabeth's uncle and Swan's master. The

28 MARCH

THE AWFUL FATE OF AN INCENDIARY.

THIS Engraving represents the Entrance of the County of Essex Convict Gaol—the Place of Execution on the Morning of the 27th of March, 1829, when James Cook, a boy only 16 years of age, suffered for the atrocious crime of setting on fire the premises of Mr. William Green, of Witham, farmer, with whom he lived as Cow Boy.

The Buildings and Stacks, which are represented as burning, furnish a true picture of the lamentable destruction of property occasioned by this wicked boy.

It is a melancholy fact, that there are offenders of the same cast still abroad, who by their conduct, show, that the disgraceful end of Cook has not operated as a sufficient example, to deter them from the commission of the like heinous crime; such, however, may be assured, that justice will ultimately overtake and punish them.

tale begins on the night of 2 July 1751 at the Walthamstow home of Joseph Jeffries. All had been in bed for some time when the cry of 'Fire, thieves!' was raised. There was no fire but the commotion in the house saw servants rush into Mr Jeffries's bedroom to rouse him. He was discovered fatally wounded with a gunshot to the head and a knife gash to his throat. The finger was firmly pointed at Elizabeth and Swan by a destitute man named Thomas Matthews, who had been taken in and employed by Mr Jeffries until he was 'put back on his feet'; he had stayed on in the area afterwards. Swan and Miss Jeffries had cajoled Matthews into bludgeoning Mr Jeffries while he slept. On that fateful night, having met Elizabeth and Swan at the back of Jeffries's house, Matthews explained that his conscience would not let him do it. Miss Jeffries replied, 'You may be damned for a villain for not performing your promise!' Swan also damned him and stated he had a good mind to blow his brains out with one of the two pistols he was carrying. Swan made Matthews swear he would never speak of the matter and then he was sent on his way, and Swan and Miss Jeffries went up the stairs together. Matthews's statement was enough to secure an arrest, and other witnesses corroborated key aspects

Elizabeth Jeffries.

John Swan.

of the story. Found guilty, the pair were executed at Epping Forest. After the execution Elizabeth's body was given back to her family and she was buried at Southwark, while Swan was gibbeted as a warning to all at Buckits Hill near the Bald Faced Stag, the pub he so often frequented when alive.

1875   *Execution of 'the Purfleet Murderer'.* Richard Coates (22), a soldier in the Royal Artillery, taught at the soldiers' children's school at Purfleet. After playing with 6-year-old Alice Baughan for a while he took her to a closet, where he assaulted her and then killed the poor mite in a fit of shame and panic. Clear evidence of bloodstains led the police to Coates, whose whole demeanour gave him away. On closer inspection some of the child's hair was found on his great coat. Coates had the tenacity to wear his uniform in court but was stripped of it in prison after his conviction. Despite swearing his innocence in court, he was moved by the ministrations of the priest in the prison and made a condemned cell confession to the murder, acknowledging the justness of his sentence.   **29 MARCH**

1809   Elizabeth Pool, the wife of a Brentwood Inn ostler, went to Warley Barracks every week to sell small goods to the soldiers. On this occasion, as she set off for home in the darkening evening gloom, she was aware she was being followed. She paused, wondering whether to return to the barracks, but then quickened her pace and walked on. Soon a soldier caught up with her   **30 MARCH**

and asked where she was going so quickly. She said she was hurrying to meet her husband, who would be coming to meet her any minute, and walked on. The soldier caught her up again, threw her to the ground and ravished her. Two soldiers, alerted by her cries, came running to the scene; they quickly seized the soldier, George Nelson, who pretended to be drunk. Brought to trial, Nelson was found guilty and sentenced to transportation for life.

31 MARCH   Grim Tales of Essex

In the 1830s the Revd Samuel Hanna Carlisle greatly feared the predations of resurrectionists (otherwise known as bodysnatchers), and refused to bury his dead child in the churchyard at Havering Well, fearing the body would be stolen. He personally carried the body home and had it embalmed, keeping the coffin in his hall. Another dead child was preserved in one of his bedrooms for a number of years.

Churchyard watch house at Wanstead. From here a lonely vigil would be kept over the graves of the recently buried to avoid raids by bodysnatchers.

APRIL

Two 'old sweats' share tales of shot and shell.
John Cole, aged 51, a soldier of Waterloo, died on 10 April 1836 at North Benfleet. 'At the celebrated command, "Up Guards and at 'em", he was wounded by a musket ball but heroically preserved until victory.' Despite receiving medical attention in the field, the musket ball remained in him, to no ill effect, for the rest of his life. He bequeathed his medal to the curate, who erected a tablet in memory of him in the parish church.

1 APRIL   Grim Tales of Essex

A tale of dubious antiquity tells how the Devil came to Runwell Church during the middle of a Sunday sermon in about 1250. The elderly vicar, Radulphus, leapt from the pulpit and ran to the church door pursued by his black enemy as the parishioners remained frozen in terror in their pews. Radulphus slammed the great door and the Devil in his haste was unable to stop, crashing into the door and leaving his claw marks for all to see to this day. Radulphus, however, was never seen again. When the porch was examined a patch of bubbling sulphurous liquid was found where the vicar was last seen. At the centre of the puddle was a flint that was said to bear a resemblance to the lost cleric. This was removed and reverentially placed

The door and porch of Runwell Church, where the 'sulphurous liquid' and flint were found.

The Devil's claw marks on Runwell Church door.

in the south wall of the church with an inscription around it reading, 'The wages of sin is death.' The flint has now been removed to a priory. The problem with the story is that the door said to bear the marks of the Devil was erected several hundred years after the event. Perhaps the rector at the time of the replacement requested the marks to be copied onto the new door as a warning to others? We shall never know for sure . . .

Leechcraft and Cures of Essex Cunning Folk
2 APRIL

If a person or animal has been scratched or cut by a metal object, anything from a pin to a scythe, it is said to be highly efficacious to grease the offending weapon as well as the wound and then either throw the offending implement away or not use it until the wound is completely healed.

3 APRIL

1875   Thomas Johnson, 'a lunatic' committed to trial for the murder of his father and mother at Fordham, near Colchester, was confined to the infirmary at Springfield Gaol. It was recorded, 'He makes the building echo with his wild shouting and singing of scraps of songs and hymns.' It was further stated that 'he will probably be declared a lunatic in a few days and will then be removed to an asylum'.

4 APRIL

1851   PC Samuel Duce had a remarkable escape when he was attacked while trying to arrest two men he caught raiding a shop. The knife which was thrust at him hardly touched his skin thanks to his fine flannel waistcoat. The men made off but they left behind some useful clues, notably a wooden hand with a glove still on it. This false appendage led police to apprehend a one-handed poacher named Holden for his involvement in the crime.

5 APRIL

1895   Alice Hammond (21) of Ugley committed suicide by cutting her throat. In the days when suicide and attempted suicide were against the law and carried great shame for the family, the kindest verdict of any inquest was to claim the victim was suffering from 'temporary insanity' – and this was the verdict passed by the inquest on poor Alice.

Grim Tales of Essex
6 APRIL

In the 1840s the Coggeshall Gang was a band of violent thieves who became notorious across the Essex countryside. The gang leader was William Crow, an ostler at the Black Horse on Stoneham Street in Coggeshall. The gang was not above using guests' horses from the pubs' stables for its night-time escapades! After increasingly near misses evading capture, the gang went on the run. Crow was finally arrested as he was boarding a steam packet bound for America. Two other members of the gang were tracked to Liverpool by constables from Witham. Most of the leading gang members were captured and brought to justice. One was sentenced to death and others sent away for various periods of transportation; Crow was transported for life. One gang member was brazen enough to return to Coggeshall after his period in the penal colony. He had done well, by legitimate means, and lived the rest of his life in comfort.

7 APRIL **1914** *Fire at Chesterford.* A spark from a steam lorry caught hold at Bordeaux Farm and the flames, fanned by the wind, soon spread to Manor Farm and up the village street. Fire engines from Saffron Walden, Great Chesterford, Sawston and Audley End all attended but despite their best efforts by the time the fire was dampened down some 20 haystacks, several farm buildings, 8 cottages and 2 pubs had succumbed to the flames.

8 APRIL **1817** Eleven prisoners escaped from Moulsham Gaol, Chelmsford. The prisoners were all sentenced to death at the Spring Assizes but upon further consideration the judges had reduced the sentences to transportation. They effected their escape by dropping into the sewer through the privy in their cell, and thence into an outer privy in the yard where executions took place. From there they got away. The prisoners were all eventually recaptured, some from as far away as Stock, Good Easter and Chadwell Heath.

9 APRIL **1908** Beatrice Alger (24) was brought before Essex Quarter Sessions on a charge of felony at Chingford. The accused appeared in court in male attire, although when apprehended she had been dressed as a woman. Counsel for the defence explained that the prisoner was raised as a girl and always wore women's clothes, and the defendant had always believed, until this affair happened, that he was a woman. The judges believed Alger had no intention of disguising himself for devious purposes and ordered him to be imprisoned for one day – meaning immediate release.

10 APRIL **1739** Execution of Dick Turpin at York. Turpin was born in Hempstead, the Essex village where his parents kept the Bell Inn. Always a 'lively lad', Turpin received a common school education and was apprenticed to a butcher in Whitechapel. His improprieties, vile manners and habits did not impress his master. Friends and family tried to set him on the right course by inducing him to marry a nice girl from a good family of graziers from East Ham. It was not long before he was stealing the neighbours' cattle and soon he became involved with a gang of deer poachers, thieves and robbers who operated out of Epping Forest. After a few violent robberies the £100 reward for capture or information about the gang saw two of their number caught and hanged, and the rest split up to avoid detection. Turpin took to the road as a highway-man and soon hooked up with another 'gentleman of the road', Tom King. Their adventures have become legendary, but it should not be forgotten that Turpin was a particularly merciless and callous man not averse to torturing his victims. His fate was sealed when Thomas Morris, a servant of one of the keepers of Epping Forest, sought him out and attempted to take him in for the reward. Morris ended up being shot. But the net was closing on King and Turpin, and during a fracas with law officers in Whitechapel Turpin accident-ally shot King. After this brush with the law, Turpin fled north through Lincolnshire to Yorkshire, where he was brought before the magistrates after an incident in which he wantonly shot a landlord's cockerel and threatened to do the same to the innkeeper. Enquiries were made and he was eventually

Dick Turpin.

identified as the notorious highwayman. Once the day for his trial was set his days were numbered.

1840 The first constables of the new county police force appeared on the streets of Chelmsford on this day. The first batch of thirteen men were sworn in before the magistrates on 13 March, and further intakes followed over the next four weeks. All the candidates had to be at least 5ft 7in, under 40 years old, able to read, write and keep accounts, free from bodily complaint, of strong constitution and generally intelligent. They also had to produce character references from two people who had known them for at least five years. Trained by superintendents over a two-month probationary period, they were described as a 'fine body of men', whose selection 'reflects credit on Captain McHardy'. By the end of 1840 a total of 204 men had served in the Essex Constabulary; of these 40 had been dismissed and 26 resigned.

11 APRIL

A nineteenth-century Essex policeman.

12 APRIL, **County Gaols and Bridewells of Essex visited by Prison Reformer John Howard**
Visited in 1774, 1776, 1779 and 1782, Colchester Bridewell occupied part
of the town's ancient castle. It consisted of an entrance room with a fireplace
and a side room with a window. Opposite this were two rooms, each about
13ft square, set at a right angle to the room with the window. Cell partitions

Entrance to the cells,
Colchester Castle.

were made of iron gates to allow in light and air, but there was 'no decent separation of the sexes'. There was an enclosed court but it was little used by the prisoners. The only water supply was a well of 'fine water' which had been arched over. Prisoners were given little or no employment to occupy their time, and the wards were described as 'dark, and . . . never whitewashed'. There was an allowance of 3*d* a day per prisoner, while £2 a year was given for straw and £2 for fuel for heating. The keeper received a salary of £30 a year.

1731 William Smith was executed on this day at Chelmsford for horse stealing.

13 APRIL

Essex beliefs and omens that warn of the approach of the Angel of Death
Fires and candles presage death. A candle can predict a winding sheet for a corpse if, after the dripping wax has gathered, a strip of wax or tallow remains upright and unmelted by the flame, instead of being absorbed into the general tallow, and is noted to curl away from it; it foretells the death of the person towards whom it points. A hollow oblong cinder spat out of the fire is a sure sign of a death coming to the family.

14 APRIL

1893 A gang of men were discovered stealing grain from a farm at Purley by Police Sergeant Adam John Eves. They were not about to come quietly, and instead they set about the poor sergeant, beating him and cutting his throat in three places. They dumped his body in a ditch near Bell Rope Gate where it was found the following day by local carpenter Herbert Patten, who was out for a stroll with his girlfriend. Patten ran to report the foul deed to PC Chaplin at Stow Maries. A massive police investigation ensued and the horrific murder became the talk of the area and was splashed across the local press. Four local men were soon brought before the County Assizes, two of whom, brothers Richard and John Davis, were found guilty of the murder of Sergeant Eves and

15 APRIL

John Davis.

Sgt Adam John Eves. *(Essex Police Museum)*

Richard Davis.

16 April

sentenced to death. Both had previous convictions for thieving and poaching. John Davis made a condemned cell confession which exonerated his brother, so that Richard was granted an eleventh-hour reprieve. John Davies was executed on this day at Springfield Gaol by James Billington, assisted by William Warbrick.

1915 On the night of 15/16 April three German Zeppelin raiders set out to bomb the Humber. However, navigational errors led the airships astray, the mission became confused and the crews could only guess at the targets they were bombing. Two of the Zeppelins swept over Suffolk while Airship L6, under command of Oberleutnant Freiherr von Buttlar, crossed the coast at the Naze. Soldiers in Landguard Fort, armed only

with rifles, opened fire for all they were worth and acquitted themselves well; the German report on the raid stated they had damaged the Zeppelin and that its crew believed they had been under machine-gun fire! The Zeppelin dropped four high-explosive and thirty incendiary bombs over Maldon and Heybridge. A number of properties were badly damaged and a little girl was injured but luckily there were no fatalities.

17 April Grim Tales of Essex

In 1767 the post boy bringing the Norwich mail from Epping in the early hours of the morning was attacked near the Highstone at Leytonstone by a highwayman who aimed a pistol at the lad and demanded he 'stand and deliver' the mail to him. Unstrapping the bag, the boy meekly handed over the entire Norwich mail and watched the highwayman ride off into the early

morning gloom, shivering as he gave thanks for his life. A reward was offered, and Matthew Snat, a baker, was brought in but refused to plead. The Lord Chief Justice authorised the use of pressing (*see* 18 April) to force him to make a plea, and soon enough Snat declared he was not guilty. Tried and found guilty, Snat was executed and his body hung in chains near the scene of his crime as a warning to others.

Spital Road, Maldon, the morning after the Zeppelin raid of 16 April 1915.

18 APRIL

Old Punishments – Peine Fort et Dure, otherwise known as Pressing for Pleas

English courts were left in an awkward situation if suspects refused to plead. When a prisoner pleaded guilty the law stepped in, confiscated their estates and meted out punishment – frequently the death penalty. When they pleaded innocent, a trial would ensue; if found guilty, the prisoner would be punished and all his or her possessions forfeited to the Crown. If, however, the defendant chose to remain mute, then under the old laws he would remain unconvicted; he would probably be incarcerated, but his family enjoyed a degree of protection and his goods could not be touched. It was not until 1827

Pressing for a plea.

that a defendant's silence could be construed as a not guilty plea. This was a powerful incentive for many not to speak, and in response the law adopted the use of pressing to force a plea. The victim would be spreadeagled on the floor of a cell and over the course of three days weights were piled up on his chest, leaving him with the agonising choice of plead or die.

19 APRIL 1895 *Awful affair at Bradwell on Sea.* The Instance family lived on the fringes of the village at Mill End. Their daughter, just 15, had been pregnant for some months when the neighbours noticed that her condition had changed. The baby must have been born but no child was to be seen in the household. The rumours about the child were brought to the attention of PC Aaron Taylor, who went to investigate. Any pregnancy was robustly denied, and the girl's father said he would have the girl medically examined to prove it. The doctor, however, concluded that the girl had recently delivered a child and ordered her to bed. PC Taylor and PC Collins of Tillingham later questioned the girl, who admitted that whatever had 'overcome her' the previous Sunday morning had gone down the privy. The constables then set about the repugnant work of searching the cesspool but found nothing. The following day the policemen returned to search the house and the girl confessed the baby's body was hidden up the chimney beside her bed. A search of the chimney revealed a bundle containing the dead body of a female child. This was taken away and preserved in a jar of methylated spirits by Police Sergeant Spooner pending medical examination and inquest.

20 APRIL 1938 Police began enquiries into the suspicious death of Edgar William Allen (60), an antique dealer of Nelson Drive, Leigh on Sea. After a fire at his shop was discovered and extinguished, Mr Allen's body was found on the bathroom floor with a fatal wound to his throat.

21 APRIL The Second Chelmsford Witch Trial
In April 1579 the second Chelmsford witch trial was held at the Assizes. Four women were brought before the justices. Elizabeth Francis was found guilty of bewitchment

A Detection of damnable driftes, practized by three VVitches arraigned at Chelmiffozde in Effex, at the laste Affifes there holden, whiche were executed in Apzill. 1 5 7 9.

Set fozthe to difcouer the Ambufhementes of Sathan, wherebp he would furpzife vs lulled in feruritie, and hardened with contempte of Gods vengeance thzeatened foz our offences.

Imprinted at London for Edward White, at the little North-dore of Paules.

and hanged. Ellen Smith, whose mother had been hanged as a witch in 1574, was charged with bewitching a 4-year-old child who cried out as it died 'Away with the witch', while the child's mother noticed a hideous thing akin to a black dog leaving the house. Alice Noakes faced similar charges, and both she and Ellen Smith were sent to the gallows. The fourth woman was Margery Stanton, who was accused of bewitching to death 'one white gelding valued at three pounds and one cow valued at forty shillings'. The court found the indictment inadequate and since no human life had been threatened she was set free.

1884 On this day at 9.18am Essex was at the epicentre of an earthquake that was felt over a 150-mile radius – an area of more than 50,000 square miles. It lasted only a few seconds but people were shaken off their feet, hundreds were injured and a total of 1,200 houses were damaged. In Colchester a number of properties needed repair. The spire of St Peter's Church collapsed and the parish church at Langenhoe was so badly affected it had to be demolished. Extensive damage was also suffered at Layer de la Haye, Little Wigborough, Peldon, Abberton and Wivenhoe. On Mersea Island huge cracks appeared in the ground with water spouts erupting from them. Medi-cal personnel were kept very busy through the next few days dealing with the casualties, while soldiers were drafted in to help clear up and a victims' relief fund was set up by the Lord Mayor of London.

22 APRIL

Langenhoe Church after the earthquake.

1867 Frederick Watkins (23) was out walking with his sweetheart Matilda Griggs (16) at Buckhurst Hill. She had already borne him a child but they lived apart, she with her parents; he worked in London and visited her a few days each week. Now she was 16 it was expected, at least by Matilda and her family, that the pair would marry but Watkins seemed reluctant to set a date. While they

23 APRIL

were walking out together on this fine evening, he began to accuse her of flirting with other men, a charge she confidently and immediately denied. Appearing to calm down, Watkins suggested they cross over the palings into a field. Then, without warning, Watkins drew out a lead weight on a string and struck her about the head repeatedly until the string broke. He then took out a dagger and stabbed her several times. In his haste he did not realise the knife was still in its sheath. Despite this horrific attack, Matilda managed to struggle to the fence, where she was discovered a few hours later and taken home. Watkins gave himself up at Epping police station at 5.00am on the morning after the murder. Convinced he had killed her, he was surprised when he was charged only with cutting and wounding with intent to murder. By the time his trial came to court Matilda Griggs was well on the road to recovery and Watkins's parents had paid her to 'disappear' so she could not give evidence at his trial. Amazingly,

The murderous attack on Matilda Griggs.

despite everything, she still wanted to marry Watkins. However, he was found guilty of 'unlawful wounding with intent to do grievous bodily harm' and was sentenced to twenty years' penal servitude. Matilda did not wait for him. She eventually married a Leytonstone tailor, joined him in the trade and bore him three children.

1871 This day saw the first 'private' execution in Essex conducted at Springfield Gaol, Chelmsford. The activities of influential pressure groups, appalled at the barbaric nature of public executions, led to the Capital Punishment Amendment Act of 1868, which ensured that the execution of felons would henceforth take place within the walls of the gaols and prisons. Berwick-born Michael Campbell (28) was the first man to be executed within the prison walls in Essex, for murder. Campbell and three accomplices broke into a house on Canon Street in Stratford but they were disturbed by the occupant, Samuel Galloway (49), who chased the burglars off his property. Despite his courage, the burglars laid in wait for him and seized hold of him. As two of them held his arms, another struck him on the head with a blunt instrument. Poor Mr Galloway died ten days later from this blow. Mrs Galloway witnessed the attack and identified Campbell as the assailant. At his trial Campbell admitted his guilt but denied any intent to kill. Found guilty of the murder, Campbell was sentenced to death and was duly dispatched by public executioner William Calcraft.

24 APRIL

Springfield Gaol, Chelmsford, *c.* 1905.

25 APRIL **1837** *Riot at Braintree Union Workhouse.* After the early morning shift the thirty men working at the workhouse mill came in for breakfast, but then refused to return to work unless each had half a pound more bread a day and a little small beer. A complaint against them was brought before the magistrate, who sent William Larkin, William Unwin, William Dee and Jesse Gunn to Springfield Gaol for two weeks' hard labour as an example to the others. The sentencing was read out at the workhouse the following day, but far from quietening down the inmates they became more aggressive. There were fears of an outright riot, and twenty-four men (ten of them under 21 years old) were brought before the magistrate. Their principal spokesman was a man named Reed, who repeated the request for more bread and small beer, and cited the near-collapse of a young man who 'was almost dying from [want of] drinking water when he came off the tread wheel'; they had not food enough for working men, said Reed, commenting that even those who did not work were 'treated as slaves'. The magistrate stated he was satisfied the food was sufficient and he pointed out that if they had a complaint they should make it to the workhouse guardian and not refuse to work. Three boys were then sentenced to two weeks' hard labour in Halstead Gaol, and the others to various terms of imprisonment with hard labour.

26 APRIL **1848** *Escape from Springfield Gaol.* While new buildings were being erected at the prison, John Bryant and Edward Edwards were being held in an old and less secure area. Released from their cells for their daily duties, they mounted the 12ft yard wall, crossed a low roof and then dropped down between the debtors' prison and the boundary wall, using the ropes and ladders belonging to the workmen on the building site. They scaled the wall with ladders and scaffold rope, and were only spotted by servants in the chaplain's house as they made their escape across the fields behind the prison. At the same time a prison officer noticed the ladder and rope against the wall. The alarm was soon raised and men set off in pursuit but it was too late, and the fugitives were last spotted near Caton Hall . . .

27 APRIL **1919** During the night of the 26th and into the morning of the 27th high winds and driving snow, followed by torrential rain, thunder and lightning, caused the 'wildest night for years' in Essex. Trees were torn up by the roots, tiles were stripped from roofs, a man died from exposure while sheltering in Epping Forest and a young girl was swept away and drowned by surging flood waters at Mountnessing.

28 APRIL **Old Punishments: Branding**
Branding, a term derived from the Teutonic word brinnan, meaning 'to burn', was introduced by the Anglo-Saxons and used as a punishment until the nineteenth century. A red-hot branding iron was applied to the hand or face, with different letters indicating the type of crime committed, such as 'V' for vagabond, 'T' for thief, 'C' for coin-clipper, 'B' for blasphemer, 'M' for malefactor and 'FA' for false accuser. Those branded with a double 'S' (one

on either side of nose) had sowed sedition. In 1726 prisoners who could demonstrate their ability to 'read like a clerk' gained the right to be 'cold ironed'. On payment of a small sum, the branding iron was plunged into cold water before being pressed against the skin.

A pair of branding irons.

1800 In late April 1800 the *Essex Chronicle* reported a story about a Spanish sailor serving on one of the navy's gun vessels at Harwich. This man claimed that three years previously he had sold his soul to the Devil in order to escape from his incarceration in a Spanish prison – but the Devil swore he would want his man in three years' time – so he was due to appear any day. The story soon became common currency in the town and some four hundred people, including 'two dissenting ministers' who intended to block the Devil's way with prayer, gathered at the sailor's shore billet and waited for two hours for the Prince of Darkness to appear. The sailor explained later that his 'master' had missed his appointment 'owing to him being much engaged with the Corn Factors and Millers at and about London'.

29 APRIL

Colchester Castle, ancient stronghold and prison pictured *c.* 1905.

30 APRIL

Wreckage of the
crashed Heinkel
IIIE and damaged
buildings, Victoria
Road, Clacton.
(Essex Police Museum)

1940 A German aircraft crashed at Clacton-on-Sea on this day causing Britain's first civilian casualties of the Second World War. The Heinkel IIIE bomber was on a mine-laying mission when it was damaged by anti-aircraft fire from batteries near Harwich. The pilot attempted to land on some open ground near Victoria Road but the aircraft overshot and ploughed into a house, its bombload of mines exploding on impact. The blast destroyed 67 houses. The occupants of the struck house all died, as did the bomber's four crewmen, while another 106 people were injured.

MAY

The Essex police cart for the escort and transportation of rural offenders, *c.* 1910. Before the days of motorised vans and 'Black Marias', most country policemen would have to resort to walking or horse-drawn police carts and traps to escort prisoners into custody. *(Essex Police Museum)*

1 MAY   May Day was traditionally a day of celebration, with dancing around the maypole and similar festivities taking place to ensure the continued fertility of the land and good harvests. In Hitchin and other parishes across Essex the local lads, known on this day as 'Mayers', were out by 3.00am affixing may branches to the doors of many of the larger houses in the parish – the bigger the branch the more honourable (or generous) the household was regarded as by the Mayers. However, if any of the Mayers had been offended in some way by the household, then a branch of elder and a bunch of nettles were fixed to the door instead. This was considered a great disgrace and led to much ridiculing of the master of the house, his family and servants!

2 MAY

Capt J.B.B. McHardy

1844 Tragedy hit the household of Captain John Bunch Bonnemaison McHardy, the first Chief Constable of the Essex Constabulary, when his 11-year-old daughter Mary fell into the River Chelmer. Seeing her in difficulties, Emily Gace (19), the family governess, disregarded all thoughts for her own safety and dived in to help. Tragically both young ladies drowned. They were buried in the nearby cemetery of Holy Trinity Church and a fine window complete with a brass tablet recording the fatal event was erected by the mourning captain inside the church.

3 MAY   Leechcraft and Cures of Essex Cunning Folk
To cure bleeding from the nose wear a skein of scarlet silk round the neck, tied with nine knots down the front. If the patient is a male, the silk should be put on and the knots tied by a female and vice versa.

To cure bleeding from wounds repeat these words three times, desiring the blessing of God:

> Stand fast; lie as Christ did
> When he was crucified upon the cross;
> Blood, remain up in the veins,
> As Christ's did in all his pains.

Essex beliefs and omens that warn of the approach of the Angel of Death

4 MAY

The breaking of a wedding ring was regarded as a sign that the wearer would soon be a widow.

It is considered unlucky for anyone other than the proper officials to toll the death-bell. The stranger is said to ring his own death-bell.

If you overturn a loaf of bread in the oven, you will have a death in the house.

1944 An American serviceman named Lawson France reported back to his camp at Birch and disclosed he had had a fight with a civilian in a nearby field. France feared he had killed the man. He directed a search party to the scene where the dead body of Percy Charles Knock was recovered. Investigations revealed that France had been accosted by Knock in a local public house. Subsequently Knock followed France when he left the pub and walked down the road towards the camp. Eventually they had a conversation and they crossed the field, where an indecent act took place. Afterwards there was a fight during which Knock was strangled by France. At the subsequent court martial, France was acquitted of murder on the evidence presented.

5 MAY

1805 *Stand and deliver!* Mr and Mrs Richard Mulliner were heading to town in their gig from Woodford Bridge when a man strode confidently into the road, presented a blunderbuss and demanded money. Fearing

6 MAY

for their lives, the Mulliners complied, but as Mr Mulliner handed over his silver the highwayman replied, 'This will not do, sir; I must have your pocketbook likewise.' He then demanded Mr Mulliner's watch in the same manner. Satisfied that there was nothing left to plunder, the highwayman levelled his blunderbuss and ordered them to leave the scene: 'Come sir, off directly, no delay.' Later that night the highwayman attempted to rob William Attridge, but Attridge saw the felon in time, whipped up his horses and drove past at speed. The highwayman discharged his blunderbuss at the vanishing coach, the force of the explosion blowing his hat off. The following day William Robinson, a groom, was waylaid by the highwayman on Snakes Lane, Woodford Bridge; after relieving him of his money, the miscreant ordered Robinson to take the pocketbook to the White Hart at Woodford. The highwayman, eager to recoup the value of his spoils, went to London and took the watch to Mr Lee, a pawnbroker. However, his account of how he came by the timepiece did not satisfy Lee, who summoned a constable to arrest the man. The highwayman gave his name as John Bryant and in due course he was brought before the Assizes. Despite protesting his innocence, he was identified by the Mulliners and Attridge as the man who had robbed them, and was found guilty and sentenced to death.

7 MAY   1665   During this month the 'black plague' came to Essex. Fears that it was brought to the county by Londoners fleeing their plague-ridden city led to the placement of strong bodies of watchmen at the ferries and bridges to turn back any such refugees. In Waltham Abbey 23 people died, in Epping 26, in Brentwood 70, in Romford 100 and in Barking 200, but their sufferings hardly compared to the tragedy unfolding in Colchester, where an estimated 5,000 people died between May and December. There were fears that the town would be depopulated.

Old Punishments: Pinning a Suicide

At Great Wakering there is a road junction known as Baker's Grave; here a man named Clement, a baker, hanged himself from a tree and was buried nearby. Until the 1850s people who committed suicide were not often buried in consecrated ground. If they were fortunate, they were laid to rest (face down and facing west) in a separate, distant area in the north of the churchyard. Many people, however, believed that the souls of suicides would find no rest and would be forced to 'walk', harassing those they left behind. Thus such unfortunates began to be buried away from the towns and villages, usually at a four-way crossroads so the ghost would not know which path to take to return. To ensure the ghost stayed put, the body would be 'pinned' with an oak stake driven through the heart (a practice prohibited by Act of Parliament in 1823). Crowds would gather around the local sexton as he performed this duty at the wayside grave, and even children would risk the wrath of their parents by creeping along to watch the grim rite. The spirit of poor Clement the Baker still haunts the Wakering crossroads.

Leechcraft and Cures of Essex Cunning Folk

Cramp is prevented by wearing a ring fashioned from gold coffin handles; alternatively, obtaining a 'crampe ringe' blessed by the reigning sovereign was thought to be especially efficacious. In 1463 John Baret specifically itemised his cramp ring in his will, leaving it to John Brews as a valuable possession. For the less affluent folks of Essex a quick word with a knowing sort would probably result in advice to place one's boots or shoes by the bedside in the form of a tau cross, or to keep a basin of spring water under the bed. Carrying the patella (knee-bone) of a sheep or lamb also wards off cramp. It could either be carried in a pocket, the nearer the skin the better, or laid under the pillow at night. Some courageous folk who were well in with their local sexton managed to obtain human patellas, which were considered to be many times more potent.

1915 At 2.45am Zeppelin LZ38, under the command of Hauptmann Linnarz, made landfall over Southend on a reconnaissance flight ahead of the imminent attack on London. An incendiary bomb was dropped alongside the prisoner of war hulk *Royal Edward*; nobody was injured but flames estimated to be over 10ft high blasted out from the bomb on impact. Flying on to Canvey Island, the Zeppelin was hit by the anti-aircraft guns at Cliffe and turned about to escape. Ditching its bombs over Southend, it fled out to sea over the Crouch. Eleven British fighters were scrambled but were unable to catch their prey. Among the wreckage of the bomb was found a card which had apparently been dropped from the airship. It read: 'You English. We have come and will come again. Kill or cure. German.' And return they did. On 17 May a raid on Southend and Ramsgate caused more damage, with two people killed and one injured. Another raid followed on 26 May when LZ38 dropped twenty-three small high-explosive and forty-seven incendiary bombs on Southend. This time three people were killed and three injured, and once more the Zeppelin made its escape over the sea.

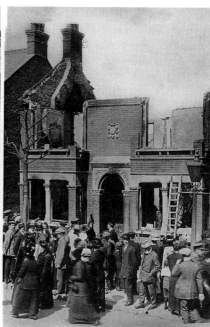

The Zeppelin air raid on Southend, 10 May 1915.

11 MAY **Last Rites**

Sam Cook died at Belchamp Walter in May 1800 aged 89 years, and his epitaph in the church reads:

Snug by the wall lies old SAM COOK
Who with his Spade, his Bell and
  Book
Serv'd Sexton three Score Years
  and Three
Until his Master, grim death, cry'd
Enough, your tools now lay aside
And let a Brother bury thee.

12 MAY **Grim Tales of Essex**

William Calcraft, Britain's longest serving public hangman, was born at Great Baddow in about 1800, the eldest of twelve children. He took up the position of hangman in 1829 and served continuously in that role for the next forty-five years. He worked all over the country, often in front of crowds of thousands. He hanged both men and women, sometimes swinging three or four at the same time in the early years of his career. He executed a number of notorious criminals, including James Greenacre (the Ratcliffe Highway murderer), Mr and Mrs Manning, Dr Pritchard, Franz Muller (the

William Calcraft.

railway murderer) and James Blomfield Rush (the Stanfield Hall murderer). He also carried out the last public execution in Britain, that of Michael Barrett the Clerkenwell bomber, at Newgate on 26 May 1868. Calcraft retired in 1874 and died peacefully at his home in Hoxton in 1879. It is estimated that in his long career he had carried out about 450 executions, 35 of them on women. Asked if he ever had nightmares or if his occupation preyed on his mind, Calcraft replied, 'As soon as I have done it, it goes from me like a puff of tobacco smoke.' The hang-men who followed Calcraft all commented on how short his 'drops' were, the condemned taking up to ten or twenty minutes slowly to strangle to death at the end of a short rope. Execu-tioners Marwood and Berry developed the longer drop and dislocation method of hanging. Marwood always said proudly: 'Calcraft hanged them – I execute them!'

County Gaols and Bridewells of Essex visited by Prison Reformer John Howard 13 MAY

Newport Bridewell was built in 1775 and was visited in 1776, 1779 and 1782. The frontage was described as 'elegant but plain', and within were the keeper's apartments and a room for the justices. Behind was the men's court with a pump in the middle; two of the keeper's windows overlooked the court to enable a watch to be kept on the prisoners. On the far side was a workroom on the ground floor with a fireplace (the only one in the prison), with a smaller workroom above. A lodging room was situated above the upper workroom. On the left side of the court were four lodging rooms, two on the ground floor and two above. Boarded bedsteads were present in all the lodging rooms. The rooms for the women were 10½ft square, and although they adjoined the men's quarters there was no communication between them. The rooms were, however, too small for the number of women incarcerated, and on one of his visits Howard found some of the women in the men's ward. There was no infirmary and conditions were grim: the offensive stench from the sewers pervaded throughout the prison. The allowance was 2lb of bread per prisoner, plus £2 a year for straw and 2 guineas for fuel for heating in the winter. The keeper's salary had increased from £25 in 1776 to £32 in 1782. Howard suggested the fitting of a latticed partition and door about 6ft from the keeper's door, which 'would prevent the prisoners from rushing out'.

14 MAY Grim Tales of Essex

A dragon 'of marvellous bigness' appeared at St Osyth. It was of similar build and description to the beast of Henham (see 27 May), but little more is recorded of this dragon. It was last sighted in 1189, when its appearance was regarded as a harbinger of doom. A short while afterwards Henry II died.

15 MAY

1801 James and Martha Basket were waylaid on the King's Highway by three men of military appearance and robbed of a silver watch, a pair of pocket pistols, a £5 banknote and a quantity of gold and silver coinage. Their assailants were later identified as James Butcher, Thomas Howard and Thomas Bishop. At the Chelmsford Assizes two other cases of similar highway robberies in April and February were brought against the men. Found guilty on all counts, they were all sentenced to death.

16 MAY

1910 *The Wennington Murder.* Frederick Foreman and Elizabeth Ely lived in an old railway carriage at East Hall, Wennington, and scratched a living as field workers on the farms around Grays. This evening the couple had been out drinking, and on their homeward walk Foreman accused Elizabeth of being with another man. A fierce row erupted and Foreman lashed out, kicking her (hard enough to break her right leg) and then beating her to the ground with a heavy willow stick, before leaving her for dead. In fact medical tests revealed she died of exposure. Foreman 'discovered' the body the following day. He claimed Elizabeth had left him on the night of the murder, but he had already told his workmates she was dead before 'discovering' the body. Further investigation revealed blood on his clothes and boots, while several witnesses had seen them drinking together on the night of the murder. Foreman was brought up at Chelmsford Assizes and found guilty of the murder. On 14 July 1910 he was executed at Springfield Gaol, Chelmsford, by Henry Pierrepoint, assisted by John Ellis.

17 MAY

1958 John George Perkins (44) was found guilty at Essex Assizes of shooting dead William Leyland, his neighbour, after an argument over Leyland's chickens which kept straying into Perkins's garden. Evidence was presented that Perkins had a history of mental illness, and the plea of diminished responsibility was accepted. Perkins was sentenced to life imprisonment.

1885   James Lee (alias Menson, alias Adams) (45) was executed on this day for the murder of Inspector Simmons near Romford on 20 January 1885. Inspector Simmons and PC Marden were on patrol in a horse-drawn trap. Near Rainham station PC Wilderspoon informed them he had seen three men getting off the London train, one of whom he recognised as the notorious local criminal David Dredge. Simmons and Marden immediately set off in search of the three men and found them near the sewage farm on the road towards Rainham. Recognising Dredge, PC Marden got out of the trap and challenged him, saying, 'What are you doing over here, David Dredge?' Dredge replied

James Lee.
(Essex Police Museum)

by pointing a revolver at the constable and saying, 'I'll blow your brains out with this'. Suddenly there was a loud bang as a gun went off, and the taller of the other two men was seen to be holding a smoking revolver that was aimed at Inspector Simmons. The men then ran off, with PC Marden in pursuit; Inspector Simmons, although shot in the groin, also attempted to give chase. A number of further shots were fired at the policemen and the suspects got away, while poor Inspector Simmons died of his awful wounds a few days later. Dredge was subsequently arrested in Burdett Road, Limehouse, and brought back to Chelmsford; he was soon joined by another of his criminal confederates, James Menson. Menson, who had recently changed his name to Lee (after John 'Babbacombe' Lee, 'the man they could not hang'), was found guilty of firing the fatal shot. Menson's faith in the name Lee proved misguided; cursing the legal system and protesting his innocence to the very end, Menson was duly dispatched by public executioner James Berry. Dredge was found guilty of firing at PC Marden, and was given a prison sentence with hard labour. The third suspect, one John 'Jack' Martin, remained at large for over a year but was eventually captured with two other members of a London gang who had conducted a burglary at Netherby Hall, Cumberland. They were caught at a police checkpoint at Kingstown; in trying to shoot their way out, they killed a policeman (*see* 8 February) and all three were subsequently executed.

19 MAY **1536**   Queen Anne Boleyn, the second wife of King Henry VIII, was executed on this day on Tower Green at the Tower of London. It is said that Henry was preparing to hunt in Essex when the execution was carried out. The firing of a gun signalled that the queen was dead, at which the king exclaimed, 'The business is done! Uncouple the dogs, and let us follow the sport!' Essex folklore tells how the repentant executioner, who had been brought especially to England at the queen's request to decapitate her by sword, passed through the county on his return journey. Bizarrely he had her head with him, and when he reached the parish church of East Horndon he saw to it that it received due burial within its walls. It is said to remain there to this day, but its precise location is not known.

Queen Anne Boleyn.

20 MAY **1840**   Constable Charles Calcraft, the Little Baddow policeman, was dismissed from the force after 'leaving his guard [beat] with a prostitute'. His career on the force had been a short one, lasting just nineteen days, and was the more remarkable because he was appointed as a constable not long after completing a short sentence at Colchester Gaol. Perhaps his employment was part of an early police initiative to employ thieves as thief-takers, or perhaps his appointment had been made after his brother, the public executioner William Calcraft, pulled a few strings?

21 MAY **1716**   The entry in the manor court rolls of Coggeshall for this day states: 'It was ordered that William Cox, William Clark and Mark Belsham Grimes, who at this court were appointed constables of this leet for the year following,

well and sufficiently repair the stocks and cage being within this leet within forty days after notice thereof, under pain of forfeiting to the Lord in default thereof, £5.'

Old Punishments: The Cage

Until 1840 every parish was required by law to provide a 'lock-up' or cage for the temporary detention of prisoners arrested by the parish constable. These were usually small wooden and brick structures about 8 or 10ft square, built on waste ground in a public part of the village, often in close proximity to the stocks and whipping post. A number of cages and lock-ups still exist in Essex and good examples may be found at Great Bardfield, Bradwell on Sea and Canewdon. Bradwell cage was the last to fulfil its official purpose, when it was used to incarcerate 'a suspicious-looking foreigner' who had wandered into the village during the spy scares of the First World War.

Great Bardfield cage.

Grim Tales of Essex

Raphael Holinshed recorded in his *Chronicles of England, Scotland and Ireland* (1577) an unusual visitor to Danbury in 1402: 'On Corpus Christie daie at evensong time, the Devil appeared in a towne in Essex called Danburie, entring the church in likeness of a greie friar, behaving himselfe veries outrageously, plaieng his parts like a devil indeed so that the parishioners were put in a marvellous fright. At the same instant, there chanced such a tempest of wind, thunder and lightning, that the highest part of the roofe of the church was blown down, and the chancel was all to shaken, rent and torne in pieces.'

The Devil disguised as a monk, about to attack a priest.

24 MAY **1611** Martha Warde was delighted to have secured a position as a maid in Saffron Walden and set out on this day from her home in Chelmsford as a passenger in a carrier's cart loaded up with large bundles of linen. Roads were far from well made in those days, and turnpikes were still in the future, so as they trundled along the cart was thrown from side to side by the uneven road surface and countless potholes. During the journey some of the bundles collapsed onto Martha; unable to get free or call for help, she was only found when the wagon was unloaded. She was blue in the face and quite dead, having suffocated among the bundles.

25 MAY **Essex Witches and Witchcraft**
A clergyman at Laindon was said to be a wizard, who was assisted by three imps. He told his servant the imps would never hurt her but that she should never take a light into his room. The existence of the imp familiars was attested to by a number of people. Two were described as

Witches and imps on their sabbat.

being like moles and the other like a cat. When the clergyman died, nobody could find them or knew what happened to them.

1870 Martha Finch was found dead in bed with her throat cut at the home she shared with her husband and family at Sandon. Her husband Isaac was missing, and a search soon discovered him wandering in the fields. When he realised he was being pursued he threw himself into a ditch but as the searchers approached he climbed out and went quietly with them. In his pocket was found a Bible with a leaf marking the page describing how David stood upon the body of the Philistine, took out his sword and cut off his head. In the coalhole of the house was found a blood-stained billhook, undoubtedly that used to kill Martha. Finch was taken into custody and stood trial for murder at the Summer Assizes. It emerged that his family had a history of mental illness, and Finch himself had been in a state of deepening depression. It was related in court that he had left the Church of England to join another sect known as the 'Ranters'. Mrs Finch had been worried about him, and confided to friends that the way Isaac 'turned up his eyes' had made her feel 'quite ill with alarm'. Found not guilty of wilful murder on the grounds of insanity, Finch was ordered to be detained 'during Her Majesty's pleasure' and was removed to Broadmoor.

26 MAY

1669 A contemporary pamphlet published by Peter Lillycrap claimed that a flying serpent was seen for the first time on this day when it darted out in front of a horseman; he observed that at 'divers times [it had] been seen at a parish called Henham-on-the-Mount, within 4 miles of Saffron Walden'. He cited reliable witnesses such as churchwarden Richard Jackson, parish constable Thomas Presland and even John Knight, an overseer of the poor. Two locals even claimed to have observed the beast as it lay sunning itself on a hillock. They estimated it was some 9ft long, tapering in girth from about the size of a man's thigh down to about the size of his leg. Its eyes were said to be akin to those of a sheep, while a set of fierce teeth lurked behind its thin lips. The two stubby wings that protruded from its back hardly looked substantial enough to enable it to fly. A number of brave men attempted to shoot the creature down with arrows and matchlocks, but to no avail, as it swiftly took cover in the woods. Then one day it was nowhere to be found, having vanished as mysteriously as it had appeared.

27 MAY

An Essex dragon pew end.

Essex Witches and Witchcraft

28 MAY

In 1880 father and son Charles and Peter Brewster of High Easter accused Susan Sharpe, the wife of a local labourer, of being a witch and of having bewitched Peter Brewster's wife. The matter was taken so seriously by the Brewsters that they brought an action before the magistrate in an attempt to obtain an order to 'swim' Mrs Sharpe in the village pond to see if she really was a witch. Father and son were admonished by the bench for their 'very foolish act', and each was bound over in his own recognisance of £5 to keep the peace for six months.

Leechcraft and Cures of Essex Cunning Folk

29 MAY

From 1723 Dr Benjamin Allen of Braintree kept a notebook of his remedies, which clearly demonstrate that some 'trained' physicians at that time were little better than cunning folk! For jaundice after ague he suggested a spoonful of powdered peacock dung in a bitter drink. Tuberculosis was treated by a draught of sheep dung fermented in a pint of milk overnight. Those unfortunate enough to be bitten by a mad dog were advised to catch and kill the dog, cut out its liver, fry it and eat it.

30 MAY **1953** George James Newland (21) considered himself to be in desperate need of a new suit but, like so many young men in that position, he lacked the money to buy one. Instead of saving for his dreams and ambitions, he wanted the money there and then and hatched a despicable plot to obtain it. During his National Service he had been stationed at Orsett, near Grays, where he had befriended an elderly couple named Tandy who lived in a nearby bungalow. Taking with him some apples and oranges, he set out to visit his old friends. On the way out he also picked up his father's claw hammer and slipped it into the same bag. Turning up on the Tandys' doorstep, he was welcomed in like a lost son, but after catching up on old times Newland took out the hammer and set about the elderly couple with it. Mrs Honor Tandy was clubbed down and rendered unconscious (she recovered after a long stay in hospital), while Mr Henry Tandy was beaten to death. Newland left the house with just £8 5s. He was soon traced and taken into custody. He admitted the crime, claiming he had been inspired by a violent film. Found guilty, he was dispatched by executioner Albert Pierrepoint and his assistant Harry Allen at Pentonville on Wednesday 23 December 1953.

31 MAY **Grim Tales of Essex**

Osyth was the daughter of Frithewald and Walburga, the first Christian king and queen of the East Saxons. After enduring marital strife, she founded a nunnery and eventually became its abbess. In about 870 the religious buildings were attacked by Danish raiders. Osyth attempted to shield her nuns from the raiders but they cut her head off. Miraculously she picked it up again and walked 3 furlongs to the church where she struck the door with her bloodstained hand to indicate she should be buried there; only then did she fall down and die. The decapitated head of the sainted abbess was kept as a revered relic in a silver casket at St Osyth's Priory until the Dissolution, when it disappeared. The spirit of St Osyth is said to walk once a year, head carried in her hands, at the scene of her martyrdom, a holy well in Nun's Wood.

St Osyth depicted in stained glass.

JUNE

Ancient oak of Stapleford Tawney, near Epping, struck by lightning, 28 June 1813. Some of the scattered pieces were thrown 100 yards from the tree; one piece, weighing 'over half a hundredweight', was thrown a distance of 60 yards.

1 JUNE **1884** *The 'Whitsun Murder', Newport.* The Blyth family had lived on Church Street in Newport for just a few months. Emily Blyth (26) said her husband Charles (33) was a travelling jewellery salesman and bookie. He was frequently away on business, so they had moved to Newport so his wife could be closer to her mother. Emily said she would be glad of another pair of hands to help with her two young children, especially as there was another on the way. Early in the morning of this day a heavy bump on the wall alarmed the Blyths' neighbour, George Gayler, a baker. He went to tell William Newell (Mrs Blyth's brother), who lived a few doors away. Newell hurried to the house and to his horror discovered that Charles Blyth had shot and killed poor Emily. Gayler summoned the police and Blyth was arrested by PC George Sawkins, assisted by John Buck, a retired Metropolitan policeman who lived nearby. Investigations revealed that Charlie Blyth had only recently been released from a stay in London's Bedlam Hospital, where he had been incarcerated for attempting to take his own life, and was 'not safe'. The truth was that Emily had moved to Newport partly to be near her family and partly to get away from Charles, whom she thought would end up in the sanatorium permanently. Charles Blyth was sent to Broadmoor Hospital for the criminally insane for the rest of his life.

2 JUNE **1801** John Hight, Henry Harding, William Warley, James Butcher and Thomas Howard, all soldiers in the 1st Regiment of Guards, decided to go on a night-time burgling expedition to the home of Mr Thomas Blyth of Langham. Entering the house armed with pistols and a battleaxe, they pressed two pistols to the heads of Mr and Mrs Blyth and demanded their valuables. After ransacking the house they got away with a canvas purse containing 40 guineas, one £5 banknote, divers other monies, a silver watch and three silver tablespoons. Apprehended soon afterwards on suspicion of other felonies, all five soldier-burglars were brought before the Assizes, found guilty and sentenced to death.

3 JUNE **1846** George May Smith (18), a 'genteel-looking lad', approached his former employer, Thomas Woodcock Warner of Thaxted, for a character reference. Warner, who had discharged Smith for 'misbehaviour', refused to give him one. Annoyed, Smith deliberately discharged his shotgun at Warner but it exploded, severely injuring Smith and only slightly wounding Warner. At the Assizes Smith plea-bargained and admitted intent to cause grievous bodily harm. It was a narrow escape from the noose – he was sentenced to transportation for seven years.

4 JUNE **The Witches of St Osyth**
In 1582 the witches of St Osyth were tried at Chelmsford. Thirteen women stood accused, ten of them on charges of 'bewitching to death'. It seems that the usual rules of evidence did not apply in these trials and the testimony of children aged between 6 and 9, some of whom could well have been hysterical, was eagerly received and accepted as fact. Six women were found

guilty and sentenced to death but only two actually went to the gallows, Ursula Kemp and Elizabeth Bennett, who had confessed to killing a man and his wife by witchcraft. Kemp was indicted for three deaths by bewitchment between October 1580 and February 1582. She eventually confessed and was found guilty on all three counts. In 1921 the skeleton of a woman was found in a garden in Mill Street, St Osyth. Careful excavation and examination revealed she had been 'pinned' to the ground with iron spikes through the joints. This was an ancient practice said to stop the witch's spirit 'walking abroad and causing mischief'. It was widely believed to be the skeleton of Ursula Kemp, and coachloads of tourists came to gaze into the open grave. Curiously, the house in whose garden the skeleton lay was burnt to the ground in 1932. Locals were concerned it was the witch's doing and had the grave filled in. In the 1950s the skeleton was removed to the witchcraft museum in Boscastle, Cornwall.

The 'pinned' skeleton believed to be the remains of Ursula Kemp found at St Osyth, 1921.

1813 *The Murder of Martha Stevens.* Martha Stevens, keeper of a chandlery shop at Woodford, was not seen on Sunday 6 June and by Monday the 7th concerned neighbours effected an entry to her house through the bedroom window. The bed did not appear to have been slept in and when they moved on into the shop her body was found lying face down on the floor with her throat cut. Burglary was the obvious motive. Suspicion fell on William

5 JUNE

Cornwell, a lodger at a nearby property. Known to be always short of money, he had returned to his lodgings late on Saturday night with enough money to pay for a trip to London and a few expensive purchases. His fate was decided when a description of some of the stolen items was circulated and the wife of the landlord of the Sun Inn in Lincoln's Inn Fields recognised the murdered woman's watch as the one Cornwell had bartered with her husband. Cornwell claimed he had found the watch but the jury at his trial was convinced by the circumstantial evidence and found him guilty; the sentence of death was pronounced. With a convulsive grin, Cornwell said, 'Thank you, my Lord and Gentlemen', upon which he was removed from the bar.

6 JUNE   1945   Eva Rosemary Lucas (17) returned after a night out to the home she shared with her mother and father at Undercliffe Gardens, Leigh-on-Sea. To her horror she discovered both her parents had been battered to death. There were few leads for the police as to who had committed this horrible crime, until Mrs Wheeler of Barking informed the police of her concerns about her brother, John Riley Young. He had been staying with her since the 7th, when he was seen to have an unusual amount of money. Since then he had twice attempted to commit suicide, once by slashing his wrists and the second time by gassing himself. When he had been removed to hospital after attempting to gas himself, Mrs Wheeler spoke to the police. When they arrived on the ward Young greeted the officers with the words, 'I have been expecting you. It was me and I want to get it off my chest.' Brought to trial, Young was found guilty of the murder of Fred and Cissie Lucas and was executed by Albert Pierrepoint at Pentonville on Friday 21 December 1945.

7 JUNE   Leechcraft and Cures of Essex Cunning Folk
To cure epilepsy: in the case of an unmarried woman, she must beg from nine bachelors as many silver coins – generally threepenny bits – which were made into a ring and worn by the sufferer on the fourth finger of the left hand. To cure a man, 'maidens must supply the needful'. A ring made from a half-crown from the communion offertory is also worn for the same purpose. The blood of a live mole dripped onto a lump of sugar and swallowed was believed to be a good treatment for fits.

8 JUNE   Essex Witches and Witchcraft
The parish of Canewdon was once famous for its witches; folklore stated there were a total of 'six, three in silk and three in cotton'. There was much speculation over the identity of the 'three in silk' at any one time. They had to be well off, and over the years suspicion fell on the lady of the manor, the butcher's wife and even the wife of the parson! When one of the six died it was said a stone would fall from the church, but there would always be another witch who had been groomed to fill the vacancy.

9 JUNE   1878   Charles Revell and his wife Hester dined with her parents at their home at Fair Mead Bottom (otherwise known as Whitehorse Plain) on the

Canewdon Church,
c. 1900.

fringes of Epping Forest. The situation was strained as the Revells' marriage
had been tumultuous and Hester had been living with her parents for some
weeks. After the meal Revell went to a public house for a drink. After some
time Hester went after her errant husband and brought him back to the
house, where a row broke out. She accused him of taking 3s belonging to

her, and then she grabbed his collar, tearing it as she did so. Revell pushed her down, left the house and stormed off into the forest. Hester followed him. She was found the next day with her throat cut from ear to ear. Revell was a prime suspect. Only days before the murder he had had his razor sharpened and when he collected it he cursed his wife and said, 'There'll be a murder in the Forest before long.' Even when he was apprehended, he declared: 'Good luck to her; a good job; and the sooner a rope is about my throat the better.' At his trial the jury were only too happy to oblige, returning a firm verdict of guilty; sentence of death was pronounced. Revell was executed at Springfield Gaol on 29 July 1878.

10 JUNE   1851 The vigilance of the policemen observing the home of Mr Cook at Twinstead (Great Henny) paid dividends when three men were spotted 'burglariously' entering the premises. They were soon followed by Constables John Eldred, John Jonas and William Humphrys of Essex Constabulary and PC Cross of Suffolk Constabulary. When the lawmen challenged the intruders, one of the policemen was immediately struck down by one of the burglars with a blow from a chisel. Another robber was tackled by John Flower, one of Mr Cook's labourers. All hell broke loose and a desperate struggle ensued; fists and weapons flew, and eventually a shot was fired (which resulted in the amputation of John Flower's arm). So much blood was spattered about that the officers who examined the scene described it as a 'slaughterhouse'. All the intruders were eventually brought in and identified as Stephen Pryke, William Poole and James Dawson. Poole's head had been badly cut in the mêlée and he died of his wounds soon after. Dawson was sentenced to death (later commuted to imprisonment) and Pryke was transported for ten years.

11 JUNE   **County Gaols and Bridewells of Essex visited by Prison Reformer John Howard**
Halstead Bridewell was visited in 1776, 1779 and 1782. The house was rented from the Trustees of Martin's Charity. Men and women had separate workrooms and lodgings, and there was also a room for the sick; all these rooms required repair. There was one court, used by the men during part of the day and by women for the rest of the time. There was no source of water. The keeper was paid a salary of £32. Prisoners were allowed 1½lb of bread and a quart of small beer a day. The prisoners were occupied in spinning but were not allowed to retain any part of what they earned. Halstead Bridewell was burnt down in March 1781, four prisoners perishing in the flames. On Howard's last visit another prison was being built nearby on a patch of ground that had been purchased by the county.

12 JUNE   1903 Downpours of torrential rain started on this day and continued incessantly over the next ten days, causing rivers and waterways to burst their banks. There were instances of flooding all across Essex. The south-west of the county was worst hit; here, hundreds of homes were rendered uninhabitable and thousands of pounds' worth of damage was caused.

Beeleigh Weir under
flood, 1903.

1648 *The Siege of Colchester.* As England sank into civil war, the Royalist   13 JUNе
army marched on Colchester on 12 June. Finding the town 'willing
to stand in opposition', one of the Royalist leaders,
Sir Charles Lucas, himself a Colchester man, promised the
town would not be sacked or plundered and they were
allowed to take refuge in the town while they awaited
reinforcements. In the meantime the Parliamentary
forces under Sir Thomas Fairfax had crossed
from Gravesend to Tilbury and rapidly
marched towards Colchester, arriving on
the 13th. They immediately ordered the
Royalists to surrender. This was refused
and so Fairfax attacked the town; the
gates were shut and defended and
thus began the siege of Colchester. It
took Fairfax six days to surround the
town, but the Royalists used the time
wisely, stocking up on what food and
goods they could for the inevitable
siege. Fairfax built considerable works
and fortifications around the town and
ordered cannon to be brought from the
Tower of London armouries; these inflicted

Sir Thomas
Fairfax.

considerable damage on the town. Despite the Royalists' brave attacks on the fortifications at night they could not lift the siege, but the inevitable shortages of gunpowder and food spelt doom for the town's inhabitants (*see* 27 August).

14 JUNE — Old Punishments: The Stocks

The stocks were probably the oldest and most widely used device for punishing minor offenders such as beggars, drunkards, louts, prostitutes and scolds. In the close-knit communities of the past, retribution against those who transgressed the social or moral codes was both public and humiliating. The simple construction of the stocks changed little since their earliest appearances in Anglo-Saxon books. They consisted of two sturdy uprights fixed in the ground, having grooves in their inner surfaces in which were slotted two solid timber boards, one above the other. Each plank had semi-circular holes cut in it which, when aligned together, formed holes that encircled the culprit's ankles. With the upper plank held in position by a padlock there was no escape for the victim until he or she was released by the parish constable, beadle or other official. The authorities considered it so important that villages should have stocks that Acts decreeing this were passed in the fourteenth and fifteenth centuries. After 1405 a village that lacked stocks and a whipping post was downgraded to the status of a mere hamlet. Used commonly into

The stocks at Havering-atte-Bower.

the eighteenth century, stocks were known to have been used for drunken miscreants up to the late nineteenth century. One of the last recorded uses in Essex was at Great Canfield in 1860, when a local man was put in the stocks for drunkenness.

Grim Tales of Essex

15 June

In 1695 John Tyrell of Billericay recorded a tale told to him by his grandfather. It related to a time when merchants from the area first traded with tribes in Africa, and they brought home with them a great serpent, which soon escaped from its cage. The beast made its lair in the woodlands between Heron and Horndon parish church, and chose weary passing travellers as its prey – swallowing them whole! Sir James Tyrell slew the beast but after the desperate struggle the good knight collapsed and died from exhaustion. A little time passed and the knight's son, still in mourning, went to the site of the battle. Discovering the bones of the serpent still lying there, he cursed them and kicked them. As he did so, one of the bones pierced his shoe, pricking his toe. The wound soon became infected and his leg had to be amputated at the knee.

1958 Albert Jarrard (49), a labourer, was brought before the Assizes charged with the murder of his son (3). His wife said she had awoken to see her husband pulling a rope around the child's neck as he lay in his cot. Dr Brisby, Principal Medical Officer of Brixton Prison, testified that Jarrard was suffering from melancholia and was insane. Found unfit to plead, he was ordered to be kept in custody during Her Majesty's pleasure.

16 June

1913 A tempest of hail, ice, rain, thunder and lightning struck north and north-east Essex. Three men were killed in Braintree when lightning struck the metal shed they were sheltering in and ran to earth through the pitchforks they were holding.

17 June

1866 Frederick Boston, a gunner in the Royal Artillery's 5 Battery, Depot Brigade, Sheerness, was formally drummed out of the ranks in disgrace on this day. Boston had deserted five times and in the course of his service had committed so many misdemeanours and crimes that he was court-martialled. He was duly turned out of the army and sentenced to eighty-four days' imprisonment in Springfield Gaol.

18 June

1903 Charles Howell (30), a soldier in the Suffolk regiment garrisoned in Colchester, had been 'walking out' for some time with a local lass named Maud Luen (19). On 1 June (Whit Monday) the couple were heard arguing and Howell had returned to barracks in a foul temper, cursing Maud and adding, fatally, 'She will not be alive in the morning.' Later that evening they met again, Maud now accompanied by her friend Mrs Tredger. Howell asked her forgiveness. Maud said she would forgive him, but that for now she wanted to be left alone. Howell put his arm around her and asked for

19 June

a kiss. Before a reply could issue from her lips there was a flash of steel in his other hand and Howell had cut Maud's throat with one swipe of his cut-throat razor. Maud died almost instantly. When a sergeant from the regiment happened to cycle by, Mrs Tredger apprised him of the situation and he took Howell to the guardroom. Howell freely admitted his deed, adding if Maud was not dead 'she ought to be'. At his trial the defence argued that Howell was insane at the time of the attack and that his mind had been affected by service in the South African War. This was an unusual defence since there was little or no concept of post traumatic stress disorder in the British Army before the First World War. The jury declared him guilty but did request a further enquiry into Howell's state of mind. However, there was no commutation of sentence and Charles Howell was executed at Chelmsford Prison on 7 July 1903.

20 JUNE   **1751**   *The Dunmow Flitch.* This custom originated in Little Dunmow and is said to have been started by the local landowner Sir Reginald Fitzwalter, who was hugely impressed by the gesture of the Abbot of Dunmow, who presented his lordship with a flitch of bacon as a reward for the kind way he treated his wife. Fitzwalter thus decreed that any man and woman who had been married a twelvemonth and a day and could swear before a special court consisting of six maidens and six bachelors that they had 'lived happily during that entire period' – and could produce reliable witnesses to back their claim – would be presented with a flitch of bacon (the side of a hog). If proved worthy, they would be carried around in the flitch chair in a grand celebration procession bestrewn with rushes, gillyflowers and herbs.

Dunmow Flitch
Procession, 1751.

1855 Constable Richard Wilkinson was ambushed and blasted by a shotgun at Stansted. The incident was believed to have been the result of 'bad blood' between Wilkinson and George Tubbs of Manuden. Tubbs was arrested and remanded at Newport police station but no further action was taken against him, so it can only be assumed there was insufficient evidence formally to charge him with the attack. Poor Constable Wilkinson had twenty-six grains of lead shot removed from his back and shoulders and permanently lost the use of his right arm. He was retired from duty on half pay.

21 JUNE

1944 Private Arthur Henry Jones (22), a soldier for less than three months, stole money from a comrade's locker and deserted from his battalion at Colchester. Armed with a Sten gun and two fully loaded magazines he went on the run. Captain Samuel Grundy (57), a regular army officer attached to the 18th Battalion, Essex Home Guard, had left the Battalion headquarters at Bull Farm near Abberton for a spot of rabbit shooting when he encountered and challenged the runaway. A struggle ensued but Jones managed to break away and run off. Captain Grundy pursued Jones over a quarter of a mile and finally caught up with him again. A second, more desperate, struggle took place that only ended when Jones shot Grundy dead with a short burst from his machine-gun. Jones soon regretted his hasty actions, contacted the police and led a detective to the murder site. His defence counsel at his trial was eloquent and it emerged that Jones had spent three weeks in a mental institution after a violent episode in 1938. These two factors undoubtedly saved him from the gallows and a verdict of man-slaughter was returned. Jones was sentenced to fifteen years' penal servitude.

22 JUNE

1853 On a small green in the village of Earles Colne stands a most handsome water pump. Similar in appearance to a wayside cross, this pump commemorates not an event, but rather the absence of one. It was erected in 1853, when the horrors of cholera stalked communities across the country. The disease did not enter the water system of Earls Colne, so local benefactress Mary Gee paid for this new pump 'in thankful commemoration for the absence of cholera'.

23 JUNE

The Earles Colne 'cholera pump'.

Essex Witches and Witchcraft
George Pickingill, the last Witchmaster of Canewdon, took over the position when Cunning Murrell died in 1860. Known to most locals as

24 JUNE

George Pickingill,
last Witchmaster of
Canewdon.

simply 'Old George', he came from a long line of Romany sorcerers. It was believed he had sold his soul to the Devil and had a parchment to prove it! At night if you dared creep up to his cottage you could just catch a glimpse of George dancing with his white mouse familiars, their eyes glowing like red rubies by the light of his hearth. If you stayed long enough you could see the furniture, including the clock, joining in the dance with them! He earned his living as an itinerant horse dealer and occasionally worked on the land – or rather, it was said, his imps did and they would mow a field in double quick time as Old George sat in the hedge smoking his pipe and drinking harvest beer by the flagon. He would summon his coven by blowing his wooden whistle and they would meet in St Nicholas's churchyard. Here they would dance naked by moonlight or firelight and 'utter incantations of mischief'. When a less tolerant new incumbent came to the church he heard the chanting and observed figures dancing by flickering firelight. Arming himself with a Bible and a riding crop, he strode into the churchyard to challenge the witches. He found nothing there, nor was there any evidence of a fire or footprints, just thirteen white rabbits half hidden by gravestones. Old George met his end in 1909 when he was said to be 105 years old. (The 1901 census records a George Pickingal aged 95 at Hockley, Canewdon.) While out walking on a dull and windy day he was strolling by the churchyard wall when his hat was blown over among the gravestones. As he climbed over to retrieve it, the sun broke momentarily through the clouds and cast the shadow of a headstone in the shape of a cross over George's face as he stooped to pick his hat up. It killed him instantly.

1901 George Facer (47) and Jeannie Tait (32) had lived together as man and wife for about fifteen years, but they had been estranged for about eighteen months. Jeannie had placed their two children in the Dr Barnardo's Home for Waifs and Strays and moved to Southend. Attempting a reconciliation 'for the sake of our children', Facer came to visit Jeannie there. Melora Cummings, a witness at the inquest, stated that she saw Facer confront Jeannie near her home on Honiton Road. They argued, and he grabbed hold of her. When she struggled he pushed her to the ground – and then he pulled out a revolver from his pocket. Jeannie screamed 'Don't, Don't' but Facer fired twice at her at point-blank range. He then put the pistol to his ear and fired, before firing another shot into the air. He then put the gun to his ear again but it would not fire. Although wounded, Facer outran the witnesses and a police officer and finally succeeded in shooting himself in woodland near Thorpe Hall, Southchurch. A number of letters written by Facer claimed that he and Jeannie had entered into a suicide pact; other letters praised her and said he was the cause of their separation. They also outlined which property from the marriage was hers. All these letters were presented at the inquest. The verdict of the jury was clear: Jeannie Tait was wilfully murdered by Facer, who committed suicide while in a state of insanity.

25 June

Five pairs of twins at an Essex children's home.

26 June   **1856**   A letter was received by the town clerk of Harwich asserting the author's disgust at seeing the Chief Constable of Harwich Police, in full uniform, attending an illegal prize-fight between two bare-knuckle fighters at Bentley on 17 June. The letter asserted that the crowds, which had come on a special train from London, were dispersed and escorted back to Bentley station by a large turnout of county police; among the crowds was the Harwich Chief Constable! Asked to explain himself, Chief Constable Coleman swore he had acted on intelligence and 'decided to set off in pursuit' but when he arrived he found the county officers already there and only remained to assist them. When asked why he had clambered onto the train with the crowd, he explained it was because he had begged a lift in the brake van as far as Manningtree in order to catch the connection back to Harwich.

27 June   **1885**   Saffron Walden police issued handbills and posters seeking the mother of a new-born female child whose body had been found in some bushes by the side of the Littlebury Road by a young girl named Ada Halls. Despite extensive local enquiries, the mother was never traced and the tiny baby was laid in an unmarked grave.

Church Street, Saffron Walden, in the late nineteenth century.

1962 Brian Abbott (16), a tea boy, was brought before the Assizes accused   28 JUNE
of murdering Albert Crabb (46), the storekeeper at the place where Abbott
had previously worked. Mr Crabb had been hit with a hammer, robbed of
£15 and his body set on fire. Abbott's mental state and immaturity were
brought into question; he was found guilty of manslaughter and sentenced to
be detained at Her Majesty's pleasure.

1847 Mr Ketcher, a respectable farmer of Ratsboro' near Southminster,   29 JUNE
had just set out to return home after visiting Mr Grice at Asholdham when
he spotted a man in a field where he knew there was no footpath. Aware
he had been seen, the man tried to conceal himself in the corn. Ketcher
went over and challenged the man, receiving 'an impertinent reply';
challenged again, the man lashed out and beat Mr Ketcher about
the head with a wine bottle, causing a number of 'frightful gashes'.
One wound was 3in long and had penetrated to the bone; this rendered
Mr Ketcher insensible. The man then ran off. When Ketcher came round
he managed to stumble back to Grice's. A doctor was called and the
police summoned. They conducted an immediate search of the locality and
found the guilty party hiding in a straw stack and covered in blood. The
man's name was Dace and he was well known to the local police. He was

committed to Springfield Gaol for three months' hard labour for lodging in the open air.

30 JUNE **1843** The *Essex Standard* reported a farm fire at High Roothing. Arson was strongly suspected. Eight county policemen assisted in the evacuation of furniture and goods from the house and the Dunmow parish fire engine arrived 'in full cry'. Hopes were raised that some of the farm buildings might be saved, but unfortunately someone cut the water hose and all the buildings were lost.

The old wooden 'cage', whipping post and village stocks at Roydon, *c.* 1905.

JULY

The Fryatt Memorial at Dovercourt was erected by the Great Eastern
Railway & Steamship Company 'In Memory of Captain Charles
Algernon Fryatt, Master of the GER Steam Ship Brussels, illegally
executed by the Germans on 27th July 1916.' As the captain of a
merchant ship, Fryatt had proved his bravery by twice ramming
German U-boats that had attempted to attack or capture his ship,
and his brave deeds had earned him national press coverage as a
hero. Despite knowing the dangers of wartime shipping, he continued
his dangerous journeys until his boat was surrounded and captured
on 23 June 1916. Escorted to Bruges, he was interrogated and went
on trial on 27 July 1916. As a merchantman or 'non-combatant', he
was not protected by the Hague Convention. Found guilty of waging
war as a non-combatant, he was shot by firing squad the same
evening.

A burning at the stake.

1 JULY   **Old Punishments: Burning at the Stake**
It is a little known fact that far more women were burnt at the stake in England for petty treason than for witchcraft. At a time when every household represented the state in microcosm and operated on strict hierarchical lines, crimes such as plotting against or killing a master, or aiding and abetting a criminal to enter the house, were classed as petty treason (in contrast to high treason where the offence was committed against the head of the state) and were punishable by burning at the stake. (The punishment for high treason was to be hanged, drawn and quartered.) This horrible punishment was last carried out in Essex in July 1735 when Margaret Onion was burnt at the stake in Chelmsford for the murder of her husband.

2 JULY   **1846** The body of PC George Clark was discovered in a wheat field near Dagenham. His wounds and the trampled crops were ample evidence of the ferocious struggle that had resulted in his death. It appeared that he had been brutally assaulted with his own police-issue cutlass, which was found near

his body covered in blood. Detectives from Scotland Yard were called in and concluded that Clark had been murdered by a suspect who mistook him for PC Butfroy, against whom he bore a grudge. Another accusation followed when it was revealed that Police Sergeant Parsons had induced other officers to lie and state he was on duty that night. Charges of perjury were brought against the police officers but the cruel killer (or killers) of PC George Clark was never brought to justice for his murder.

1767 Thomas Wood, a Billericay miller, vowed to reform his eating habits. **3 JULY** At the age of 40 he weighed 25 stone; he was known as a phenomenon for miles around, and visitors passing through the town always called in to gawp at his massive size. Such attention was not bad for business and he took the banter with a jolly smile and a kindly word for all. By the time he approached his mid-40s his weight was beginning to affect his health. He ached constantly, lost his teeth and had frequent palpitations. The rector of nearby Nevedon was concerned enough to encourage Wood to read a book about moderation and physical improvement. Wood took the advice on board and was soon shedding weight by the stone. From July 1767 he only ate a kind of dumpling made from 1lb of flour boiled in 1½ pints of milk. His weight reduced to about 11 stone, and he remained at that weight until well into old age. He died aged 63, and was buried among a number of his ancestors in Burstead churchyard.

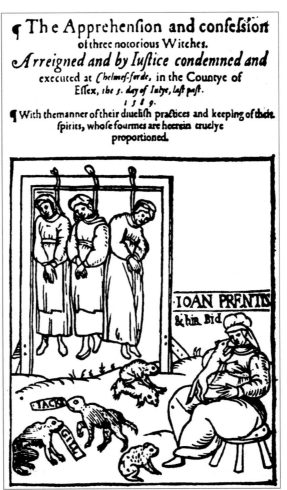

1835 Ann Child was committed to Chelmsford Gaol for having assaulted Samuel Vale, the parish constable of Rayne, while he was performing the duties of his office. Found guilty at the Summer Assizes, she was sentenced to fourteen days' hard labour.

4 JULY

Booklet page from the account of the Chelmsford Witch Trial, 5 July 1589.

5 JULY **1589** *The Third Chelmsford Witch Trial.* One man and nine women were brought to trial, most of them on charges of bewitching persons and livestock to death or of spoiling livestock and goods. Joan Cony, Joan Upney and Joan Prentice were all found guilty and executed within two hours of sentencing, all of them 'confessing their crimes on the scaffold'.

6 JULY **1878** Henry King, druggist and dry salter at Loughton, was brought before the Assizes charged with causing the deaths of four children by the sale of 'Violet Powder', which contained large quantities of white arsenic. A lesser charge accused him of selling the powder to be used for medical purposes on the bodies of children of tender years. King swore affidavits that he had never used or purchased arsenic but only starch powder; if arsenic had got into the powder, it was because his supplier had sent it by mistake. There was no evidence to indicate King had behaved maliciously, or that he had knowingly used or obtained arsenic. Public indignation pushed for a trial at the Central Criminal Court but the case was dropped.

7 JULY **1879** Frederick Brown (46), a shoemaker at Writtle, had been in low spirits since some of his household property had been seized in lieu of rent arrears. After living peaceably throughout their life together, his wife now feared for his mental state but she did not expect him to suddenly lash out at her with a hammer and afterwards cut her throat (though not fatally) with a razor. He subsequently attempted to use the razor on himself. The surgeon at the gaol stated that Brown's mind had been much weakened through drink. The jury acquitted him on grounds of insanity and he was ordered to be detained at Her Majesty's pleasure.

8 JULY **Last Rites**

A gravestone in Weeley records: 'Under this stone lie the remains of Alexander McDonald, late soldier in the First Battalion 79th Regt., who in the prime of life was inhumanely murdered near Little Clacton on the morning of the 6th July 1806.' His story is tragic. His battalion was stationed in Weeley as part of the coastal defences during the Napoleonic Wars. After a number of petty thefts and minor incidents, the grudges of assorted locals were fired by an excess of drink during the St James's Day Fair at Little Clacton. The problems were only exacerbated when the local girls seemed more enamoured with the 'kilties' than with the local boys. The soldiers attempted to gate-crash the dance at the Blacksmith's Arms but were bundled out again. The soldiers retaliated by throwing

a bayonet at the dancers and a fight erupted which resulted in the soldiers fleeing the scene. Alexander McDonald had suffered an injury to one leg and thus could not run as fast as the rest. The villagers caught this poor man near Amerells Farm and beat him to death with sticks, stones and the handle of a grindstone. Four men were tried for the murder but the evidence proved so conflicting they were pronounced not guilty.

1752   Kitty Canham was born in 1720, the daughter of a respectable tenant farmer at Beaumont Hall, near Thorpe-le-Soken. She grew into a beautiful woman but showed no signs of settling down, much to the consternation of her father. He put his foot down and made her accept the attentions of Alexander Gough, the rector, and they soon married. Kate did not love Gough and felt herself to be like a caged bird in her new life at the rectory. After a number of defiant acts and heated exchanges, she fled to London. Her beauty was acknowledged in the salons and assembly rooms, and soon she attracted a number of admirers, among them Viscount Dalmeny. He told her tales of his travels around the world and she was enraptured. When he proposed she neglected to point out her previous marriage and they were wed.

9 July

They spent four idyllic years touring the continent but it all came to an abrupt end when she became ill and died in Verona. She confessed all on her deathbed to her beloved viscount, who promptly forgave her and promised to return her remains to Thorpe. Her body was embalmed, placed in a handsome coffin and locked in a wooden chest for the journey home. At the Hythe at Colchester they encountered excise men. Reluctant to draw attention to himself and his unusual luggage, Dalmeny gave a false name. However, the customs men were dissatisfied with his answers and began opening his travelling trunks. One excise man wanted to open the coffin chest but Dalmeny protested vigorously. It was only when the man threatened to test the chest's contents by running a sword through the box that he agreed to open it. Discovering the body, they concluded Dalmeny was a murderer, but the matter was soon cleared up after a few enquiries. Gough came to Colchester and identified Kitty's body, and then threatened to kill Dalmeny. Once the whole story had been explained, Dalmeny's name was cleared and Kitty was conveyed to church in a carriage towed by six plumed horses, followed by mute mourners and her two husbands, arms linked, both mourning the death of their beautiful wife.

1899   A man named Gayner in the employ of Mr Coombes of Nelson Street was carrying out repairs on a property at 11 Prittlewell Square, Southend, when he discovered a brown paper parcel between the top of the water tank and the roof. This was found to contain the skeleton of a child, with its legs pressed behind its back and its arms across its chest. Medical examination concluded the child was a fully formed baby. Clearly the child's birth and death had been concealed. The only clue was a piece of newspaper found with the remains, bearing the date 1881. The mother's identity was never ascertained, and no one will ever know what happened to this tragic baby.

10 July

11 JULY   **Last Rites**

One of the most unusual memorial stones in the county was erected on the side of The George at Wanstead in July 1752. A cherry pie was being carried around the corner of the inn when some workmen on a scaffold repairing the wall leaned over and lifted the pie from the tray on the baker's head and ate it. The pie, intended for the parson, was duly missed and had to be paid for, but the workmen refused to do so and were sent before the magistrate who fined them half a guinea. The men were not to be beaten and cut a memorial stone into the side of the pub, which reads: 'In Memory of ye Cherry Pey as cost ½ a Guiney ye 17 of July – That

day we had good cheer, I hope to se a maney a Year. 1752.' It is signed 'David Jersey'.

12 JULY   **1913**   The GER Cromer to London Express was on its return journey to London when it collided at full speed with a light engine at Colchester North station. The driver of the local engine saw the express coming and applied full steam to try to get out of the way, but he was unable to avert the disaster. Carriages were smashed like matchwood and engine debris was strewn across

Postcard produced to commemorate the Cromer to London Express disaster.

the rails. The express train had only been in service for about three weeks; it was completely destroyed and three of its crew – Driver Barnard, Fireman Keeble and Guard Burdett – were killed. Around twenty people were injured.

1872 On this day a young farmer named Richardson was brought before the Assizes charged with a libel contained on a postcard. The card was picked up after its delivery by a servant of the house, who observed it was an imitation of a print that contained some coarse observations on the prosecutor (who was not named), 'not involving any serious imputation but rather tending to hold him up to obloquy and ridicule'. The evidence that Richardson actually sent the card was slight and he was acquitted.

13 JULY

1903 Samuel Herbert Dougal, the infamous 'Moat Farm Murderer', was executed on this day at Springfield Gaol, Chelmsford. A well-built man of military bearing, he was attracted to women – and quite a few had been attracted to him, judging by the number of offspring he left behind around the world as he served overseas with the Royal Engineers. Having already been married three times and imprisoned for forgery, he set about finding a new amour and soon settled into life with Camille Holland in Bayswater. A well-off lady with funds of some £6,000 at her disposal, not to mention a number of properties, she was the ideal prey for Dougal, who liked money as much as he liked the ladies. After their (bigamous) marriage, they purchased Coldhams Farm near Clavering in Essex in January 1899. They renamed it Moat Farm and moved in on 27 April. By 9 May Dougal had made a pass at the young servant-girl they employed, and matters were not improved by his attempt to enter her room at night a few days later. On 19 May Camille was seen by Florence the servant-girl going out with Dougal at about 6.30pm.

14 JULY

Moat Farm house.

This is a photo of the spot where the body of Miss Holland was found

Place where the body of Camille Holland was discovered.

Samuel Dougal under police escort at Audley End railway station.

She was never seen alive again. Returning home alone, Dougal spun a story about Camille going to London. Florence soon left, and Dougal rapidly moved his legal wife into the property with him. Over the next couple of years Camille Holland's bank account remained active and her assets were sold off by Dougal. But no one was quite sure what had happened to Camille. Eventually the authorities investigated, and having ascertained the irregularities of Miss Holland's finances they laid a trap for Dougal, and arrested him on 18 March 1903, initially on charges of forgery. During the investigations it was mentioned that at about the time of Camille's disappearance Dougal had been busy filling in drainage ditches around the property – and sure enough her badly decomposed body was discovered in one of the ditches filled by Dougal. She had been shot in the head. The bullet came from Dougal's own pistol. After a two-day trial he was found guilty of murder. He maintained his innocence to the scaffold. As he stood hooded and noosed awaiting the end, the prison chaplain, the Revd J.W. Blakemore, stood before him and demanded he confirm or deny his guilt before going to God. Dougal did not reply for some time, but at the last moment his muffled voice was heard to say 'Guilty'. He was then launched into eternity by executioner William Billington.

1872   Ellen Kittel, a young married woman of about 21, was indicted for the 　**15 July** murder of Elizabeth Kittel (her husband's former wife) at Great Bromley. A bright and cheerful-looking young woman, Ellen had met and fallen in love with Kittel when he worked as a labourer on her father's farm. Although he was already married and middle-aged, Ellen ignored her friends' and family's advice to steer clear of him and persisted in her pursuit of Kittel, and was heard to say several times: 'That's the man I want, and that's the man I'll have.' Her scheming took a vicious turn. The previous June Ellen had taken some beer in a bottle to Mrs Kittel, who was out in the fields. After drinking some of the beer, her children became ill and vomited. On another occasion when Ellen brought out beer, it was Mrs Kittel that was sick, but Ellen also drank some. When she vomited too, the sickness was blamed on the sloes they had all eaten earlier. Mrs Kittel was not so lucky; her condition deteriorated fast and she died on 10 June. During this time Ellen was seen to take her things to eat once or twice a day – in between times, according to witnesses, uttering expressions of hate and aversion against her. On the morning of Mrs Kittel's death, Ellen was in the house. Mrs Kittel had apparently fainted, and fallen upon something that had broken and cut her severely. At the inquest the doctor gave his opinion that she had 'died of a syncope, caused by loss of blood arising from the wounds', and the verdict was given in accordance with the evidence. Just two months after his wife's death Kittel married young Ellen – and rumours began to circulate about the circumstances of the death. Mrs Kittel's body was exhumed and arsenic was detected in her internal organs in quantities 'sufficient to have caused death'. Throughout the proceedings Ellen appeared very ill; she was heavily pregnant and a couch had to be brought into court for her. She went into labour shortly after the close of the proceedings, so the jury was discharged and her trial rescheduled. In the Winter Assizes Ellen Kittel was brought up again. This time the trial progressed but the jury were unimpressed with the evidence; they did not even leave their box before returning a verdict of not guilty.

16 JULY 1905 *The Chelmsford Mystery.* On this day Jane Carpenter (78), a lady 'on the tramp', claimed Police Sergeant Walter Peters had committed a vicious assault upon her person by kicking her between the legs after he forcefully dragged her off the Jubilee seat at the junction of Wood Street and London Road. Peters swore he had only poked her with his stick to see if she was alive. No witnesses saw the alleged assault but a few folks came to see why the old woman was screaming, and she eventually went quietly with Sergeant Peters to the workhouse. Peters reported the matter to the satisfaction of Captain Showers, the Chief Constable, but one of the witnesses, Frederick Taylor, felt his story did not quite add up and he brought a private prosecution for the 'unlawful, malicious and felonious wounding' of Jane Carpenter. When it came to court, the hearing was widely reported in the local papers as 'The Chelmsford Mystery', but as the medical evidence and the witness statements did not tally the case was dismissed. After spending the following weekend in the workhouse, Carpenter walked to Taylor's house and was driven in a cab with the blinds drawn to Shenfield station, where she caught a train to London and was heard of no more. Sergeant Peters retired from the force in 1908 with no stain upon his record.

17 JULY 1863 Francis King (alias George Smith) was brought before the Assizes for the theft of a horse worth £5, the property of his own father and brother. The horse used to be kept on Bentley Common, and was eventually found in King's possession. King made several false statements about how the horse came to be in his hands. His brother and father both gave evidence at the trial, the old man being a particularly sad and broken sight in the box; he was so overcome by the cross-examination that he collapsed in the witness-box. King was found guilty of this offence and a further charge of burglary. He had already been convicted of some similar felony and had served four years' penal servitude, committing these fresh offences as soon as he was released. This time he was sentenced to fourteen years' penal servitude.

18 JULY 1864 Emma Howard (alias Pudney), a silk-weaver, was brought before the Summer Assizes accused of the murder of her baby son, George Isaac Howard, aged 17 months. Emma lived with her parents at Halstead, and one afternoon she set out with her children to visit Mr Bunn, the Relieving Officer, to get help because she could not earn enough to support the children and herself. Emma returned from the visit without her children, and when her mother asked where they were she replied: 'I hope they are in heaven.' Further questioning elicited the information that the children were in the river; gathering her neighbours together for help, Emma's mother ran to the river and found the eldest child still alive, clinging to the branch of a

tree with his head just above the water, but the poor baby was floating, apparently dead, in the middle of the stream. Both children were pulled out by Constable Henry Young of Sible Hedingham, and the surgeon Septimus Rodick attempted to resuscitate the baby. It transpired that Emma had been suffering from severe head pains but she would not go to the chemist for medicine and the family could not afford a doctor. When evidence was presented of a history of mental illness in her family, the jury passed a verdict of not guilty on the grounds of insanity, and Emma was ordered to be detained 'at Her Majesty's pleasure'.

1898 William Wilkes, a shepherd from Canewdon, was executed at Springfield Gaol, Chelmsford. His appointment with executioner Billington arose from a stupid quarrel with his wife over some tobacco which resulted in him kicking her to death. He endured the whole legal process with doughty indifference until the day of execution loomed, when he had a physical breakdown and had to be fed. Assisted onto the scaffold, he turned to the warder and asked 'Will it hurt me?' But before the warder could reply the trap dropped and Wilkes was left to find out for himself.

19 July

Chelmsford's Shire Hall, *c.* 1900.

1861 Reports of the Summer Assizes include accounts of John Claydon (18), Charles Willis (21), William Spencer (18), William Woodham (21) and John Bunton (25), all labouring men, indicted for 'feloniously and maliciously damaging a number of trees, the property of the Dean and Chapter of St Paul's'; part of the land these trees stood on was leased to a lady named Walton and a Mr Dare. The case revealed that a field known as

20 July

Camping Close in Steeple Bumpstead had been used since time immemorial for sporting activities in the village, and the tree plantation in question adjoined this field. Believing that part of the plantation had encroached on Camping Close, the accused men had entered the trees armed with billhooks and hatchets determined to cut down the trees and reclaim the land. Mr Dare was soon on the scene, but when he tried to intervene the men expressed their determination to persevere and threatened to duck him in the pond if he interfered with them! All the accused were found guilty. Sentenced to one month's imprisonment, they were also bound over in the sum of £30 to keep the peace for two years.

21 JULY   **1835**   The sentences meted out by the recent Summer Assizes were published in the Gaol Calendar. Among the cases listed was that of tinker Charles Arnold (39), who was charged on the oaths of William Newman and others on suspicion of having received into his possession six teaspoons, a pair of silver sugar-tongs and a gold ring in the knowledge they had been stolen from Francis Taylor of Rettendon. Found guilty, he was sentenced to fourteen years' transportation.

22 JULY   **1837**   *A Day of Escapes?* On this day a large group of prisoners tried to break out of Springfield Gaol. Their plan was a simple one. They summoned the surgeon on the pretext of a prisoner being ill, and when he arrived he was escorted by a warder. The warder was immediately set upon and his keys wrested from him. The prisoners began to make their way out to the main door and freedom! The alarm, however, was raised in sufficient time for the other warders to draw pistols, blunderbusses and swords from the armoury and quell the insurrection. Reprisals were swift. Many of those who had tried to escape were flogged, some of them receiving up to fifty lashes.

Fifteen years later, in 1852, a blacksmith named Samuel Gould was taken before the magistrates at Manningtree charged with felony and was duly committed to trial. There being no lock-up in the town, Gould was chained by the leg to a post in a stable. When his escorting constable briefly left for refreshment, Gould grabbed the staple from the post and made his escape, and was last seen heading towards Colchester. Gould could not resist the fair in Colchester that Friday, but he was spotted and obliged to leave at speed. He was finally recaptured at Wix, and conveyed to Springfield Gaol.

23 JULY   **1943**   *The Bath Chair Murder.* After a motorcycle accident Archibald Brown suffered from paralysis of the spine, and his mobility had been gradually reduced over the years until he lost all movement in his legs in 1942. This, however, did not stop him from being a tyrannical husband and father who made the lives of his wife and two sons a misery through constant bullying and verbal abuse. On the afternoon of 23 July, while passing through the garden of the Brown residence in Rayleigh, their resident nurse noticed the air-raid shelter door was locked from the inside. A short while later the eldest son, Eric (19), was seen coming out of the shelter. Nurse Mitchell and Mr

The remains of
Archibald Brown's
bath chair. *(Essex
Police Museum)*

Brown set out that same afternoon on one of their regular constitutionals.
About a mile from the house Mr Brown wanted to stop and have a smoke.
Nurse lit his cigarette and after straightening the blankets moved to the back
of the wheelchair. Suddenly she was thrown to the ground by an explosion.
Still dazed but miraculously unharmed, she looked up to see that poor Mr
Brown had been blown to smithereens. The police examination of the scene
revealed that the explosion had been caused by a Hawkins no. 75 grenade
mine – an anti-tank device used by infantrymen. Eric Brown, who had
volunteered for army service, had been trained in the use of such weapons,
and indeed such mines were kept at his company HQ. When interviewed,
he appeared unrepentant and unable to comprehend he had committed
murder. He was brought before Essex Assizes, where testimony was given
on his behalf by nerve specialist Dr Rowland Hill, who had diagnosed

schizophrenia. Accordingly a judgement of guilty but insane was passed and Eric Brown was committed to a mental institution.

24 JULY **1862** James Boatman, a deaf labourer, was brought before the Assizes charged with maliciously setting fire to a haystack and a shed owned by the Guardians of the Billericay Union at Great Burstead. When Boatman was shown the charges listed on the Assizes calendar, he said: 'I did it, I was tired of working for 5d a day and a loaf of bread.' The final straw came when he was refused a pair of shoes. He was sentenced to three years' penal servitude.

25 JULY **1808** *No unions in the Army!* One case at the Summer Assizes that generated quite a stir in the local press involved twenty-six soldiers of the 28th Regiment of Foot who were charged with conspiracy. The case was centred on John O'Day (40), who 'feloniously administered in one Patrick Higgins a certain oath' purporting and intending to bind Higgins 'not to reveal or discover a certain unlawful combination and confederacy' between Higgins, O'Day and all the other men on trial. Notwithstanding the judicial preparations for the case, an order was received on the eve of the trial from the military authorities in London offering to discharge from the civil powers all twenty-six soldiers on the condition they entered into regiments on foreign service, for life. Not one refused and they were duly marched from the gaol to rejoin the colours at the New Garrison at Chelmsford.

26 JULY **1924** Elizabeth Southgate was murdered on this day by her ex-husband Frederick, not long after the couple had split up. A court order was obtained to keep him away from her, but he still insisted on attempting to enter the marital home on John de Boise Hill in Ardleigh near Colchester. An argument developed between Southgate and his wife, who turned to run away. Alas, she was too slow and Southgate plunged his knife into her back. A neighbour, Johnnie Bruce (16), bravely intervened. Southgate fled on his bicycle, but all poor Johnnie could do was cradle Bet Southgate in his arms as she died. Southgate went to Colchester and gave himself up at the mental asylum. Identified by the summons in his pocket, he was soon in custody. Despite working hard to maintain his plea of insanity and lack of memory, Southgate was proved sane and culpable for the murder of his wife at Chelmsford Assizes. He kept his appointment with the hangman at Ipswich on 27 November.

27 JULY **1926** Johannes Mommers was executed on this day at Pentonville for the murder of Augusta Pionbini. One evening, at their home in Thundersley, Augusta's sister Olive heard a scream, and roused her mother, who hurried off to investigate. She entered the kitchen just in time to catch her collapsing daughter. Blood was gushing from her neck, and she died less than an hour later. That evening Augusta had been out with her friend Johannes Mommers. They had gone for a walk and had a drink in a local pub. When

Mommers was found there was blood on his clothes and he handed over a razor to the police. He said Augusta had caused herself a minor injury with it and so he had taken it from her and gone home. Although Mommers insisted that Augusta had inflicted the wound on herself and the doctors gave evidence that the wound was self-inflicted, the jury were convinced Mommers had murdered Augusta and returned the verdict of guilty. He was duly executed for the crime.

Grim Tales of Essex   28 JULY

In the 1830s a group of farm labourers from Dorset set about improving their working conditions and attempted to set up a trade union. They were seen as a threat by their local farmers and landowners, as any notion of a union was seen as dangerous precedent, with national ramifications. As their cause began to draw attention from further afield, six of the prime movers were taken to court for their temerity under charges of 'administering unlawful oaths'. They were convicted in 1834 and sentenced to seven years' transportation to Australia. Such was the public outcry at the harsh treatment of the 'Tolpuddle Martyrs' that their sentences were commuted in 1837, but they found they were unable to resettle in Dorset because of opposition from the still-aggrieved farmers. The men and their families were granted farm tenancies in Greenstead juxta Ongar and High Laver in Essex. The land granted was not the easiest to farm, nor was it productive. There was also opposition to their presence from farmers in this locality and the tenancies were not renewed. The 'Martyrs' emigrated to Canada and started brand new lives.

Agnes Waterhouse.

1566 *Agnes Waterhouse executed for witchcraft.* In the wake of Queen Elizabeth's Witchcraft Statute (forbidding anyone to 'use, practise or exercise any invocations or conjurations of evil and wicked spirits, to or for any intent or purpose'), the first trial invoking the new law was held at Chelmsford on 26–27 July 1566. Presiding on the first day were local clergyman Thomas Cole and Sir John Fortescue, while on the second day the bench was occupied by the Attorney General Sir Gilbert Gerard and John Southcote, a Queen's Bench Judge. Three defendants appeared: Elizabeth Francis, Agnes Waterhouse and her daughter Joan, all from   29 JULY

Matthew Hopkins, two 'witches' and their familiars.

the village of Hatfield Peveril. After relentless questioning Elizabeth Francis confessed to learning witchcraft from the age of 12 from her grandmother, Mother Eve. Young Eve was allegedly granted certain powers in exchange for allowing the Devil to suckle her blood; he came to her in the form of a white spotted cat called Satan. When Elizabeth came of marrying age she asked the cat to procure the wealthy Andrew Byles as a husband for her. However, he refused her advances and the scorned witch allegedly 'willed Satan to waste his goods'; then, not content with this, 'she willed him [Satan] to touch his body, which he forthwith did and he died'. Elizabeth's second choice was

Francis, her husband at the time of the trial. During their marriage Elizabeth was accused of killing her young and noisy child by magic, and of making her husband lame by placing a toad in his shoe. Found guilty, she was sentenced by the court to twelve months' imprisonment.

Elizabeth Francis had then given the cat to her neighbour Agnes Waterhouse (63), who was charged with bewitching and killing William Fynne, 'who languished until November 1 [1565] when he died'. The court was also told she had used her magical powers to kill some hogs, a cow and three geese belonging to her neighbours, towards all of whom she allegedly bore some grudge or other. A confession of a similar deal with the Devil was extracted from her by the court, but this time the familiar appeared not in the shape of the cat but as a large toad. Agnes Waterhouse was hanged at Chelmsford on 29 July.

The third accused was Agnes's daughter Joan (18), who was charged with bewitching 12-year-old Agnes Brown, who 'became decrepit in her right leg and in her right arm'. The girl herself testified that her ailment had occurred after 'there came to her a thing like a black dog with a face like an ape, a short tail, a chain and a whistle about his neck and a pair of horns on his head'. Joan 'put herself on the country' and was found not guilty.

Ironically, almost a hundred years to the day after Agnes Waterhouse's execution, Matthew Hopkins, the Witchfinder-General, presented his thirty-two 'finds' at the County Sessions held at Chelmsford on 29 July 1645. Four of his 'finds', aged 80, 65, 60 and 40, had already died in prison before the Sessions opened. Hopkins and his team had extracted confessions from most of the poor souls there after prolonged starvation, sleep deprivation, forced walking, solitary confinement and cramped sitting, where the accused had to sit cross-legged on a hard stool for hours on end. Most of these confessions saw the accused committing malevolent acts and keeping familiars like moles, a squirrel, a yellow cat and even a mouse named 'Prick-ears'. All twenty-eight were sentenced to be 'hanged by the neck until they be dead'. Nineteen of them were 'swung' right away, five were reprieved and the rest remanded to the next Sessions. Most of those who were left were still in gaol in March 1648.

1857 This day saw the execution of Charles Finch at Springfield Gaol in front of a large crowd. Finch suffered from terrible jealousy, which caused problems between him and his sweetheart. While they were living in London, he had stormed out and gone off to the Crimea with the Land Transport Corps. On his return he sought out his former girlfriend, finding her in their native town of Kelvedon. There was a reconciliation and the relationship picked up again, but once more Finch's jealousy began to get the better of him, and the couple began to row. He stormed out again. About a week later he waylaid his sweetheart on her way to church at Rivenhall and cut her throat with a razor. Having been found guilty, Finch did not deny the crime and listened carefully to the chaplain's ministry. It is recorded that he slept soundly and ate a full breakfast before his execution, and walked firmly but 'without bravado' onto

30 JULY

the scaffold. Executioner Calcraft was up to his usual standard, and when Finch was dropped 'the wretched man struggled violently for some minutes before he died'.

31 JULY 1802 The Assizes records show us that four men awaited their fate in the condemned cells at Chelmsford on this day. Thomas Games and David Gibbons, both soldiers, had been convicted of highway robbery at Dagenham, while the others were simply described as 'Stephen Lee the celebrated gipsy and William Clarke', convicted 'for atrocious rape'. One man who had good cause to mop his brow was John Carter; capitally convicted for stealing a bay gelding in Mersea Island, he later received a reprieve.

The four members of the Essex Police who carried out the digging operations at Moat Farm, 1903. Detective-Sergeant Scott, who found the body of Camille Holland, is seated, front left, with the murder victim's dog at his feet. *(Essex Police Museum)*

AUGUST

The wreckage of Mr Simmon's balloon. On 27 August 1888 Mr Simmons the well-known
aeronaut was killed at Ulting near Maldon. He took off in his balloon, the Cosmo, with Mr
Field of West Brighton and Mr Myers of the Natural History Museum from the Olympia
Grounds at West Kensington, intending to cross the Channel to Flanders and thence to
Germany. After passing over Brentwood, Ingatestone and Chelmsford, Simmons attempted
to land the balloon but the anchor grapple failed to hold firm. The balloon crashed into some
elm trees and burst, throwing the passengers crashing to the ground like stones. All three
were badly injured, but poor Mr Simmons never recovered consciousness and died a few
hours later.

1 AUGUST **1809** John Bellars and Mary Gibson, described as 'a respectable looking man' and 'very interesting in appearance' respectively, sat in their cells at Chelmsford to await fourteen years' transportation to Australia. The previous day they had stood at Chelmsford Assizes on the capital charge of the possession of a number of forged banknotes, with the intent to pass them as genuine. Had they not pleaded guilty to the charge and been found guilty after due trial, they would almost certainly have faced the hangman.

2 AUGUST **1830** Execution of Captain William Moir at Springfield Prison, Chelmsford. The previous March Moir had discovered William Malcolm trespassing on his estate at Stanford-le-Hope. Having warned Malcolm about this on several previous occasions, this time Moir shot at him to teach him a lesson. His intention was only to wound the trespasser, and he even took the injured man to the local surgeon – but tragically tetanus (lockjaw) set in and Malcolm died. Moir was found guilty of murder and sentenced to death. Despite pleas for clemency, Moir kept his appointment with the hangman, although his body was spared the ignominy of the dissectionists and returned to the family estate for burial.

3 AUGUST **1863** *The Last Swimming of a Presumed Witch in Essex.* In a world that was making astonishing strides in technology and industry it is truly shocking to find that as late as the mid-nineteenth century the fear of witchcraft was still very strong, and in the tiny village of Sible Hedingham it resulted in the death of an innocent man. 'Dummy' was about 76 years old and lived in a fetid mud hut on the fringes of the village. He was unable to speak and communicated by means of excitable hand gestures and rough drawings in the dirt. The locals believed that his tongue had been cut out by the Chinese while he was fighting for the French. A curious character, he usually wore three different hats at the same time, and about the same number of overcoats. He eked out a simple living as a fortune-teller and charm-maker. On the night of 3 August it was a busy night in the Swan public house, where Dummy was quietly occupying his usual seat in the tap-room. Emma Smith (36), who had had a few drinks, suddenly proclaimed she had been ill for about nine months after being 'bewitched' by Dummy. She pleaded for him to remove the curse, offering him three sovereigns for his trouble. He took fright and wanted nothing to do with the matter. A crowd began to gather, and by closing time about eighty people were eagerly observing the argument. By this time Smith had had enough. She struck Dummy with a stick, and then dragged him to a nearby brook and pushed him in. She was joined by Samuel Stammers (28), a local carpenter, and the pair of them set about dunking Dummy in the icy waters. When the old man clambered out, he was immediately pushed back in by Stammers and Smith. The watching crowd uneasily told them to give it up or Dummy would 'die in a moment'. Afterwards Dummy was assisted home but he was suffering terribly after his ordeal and was taken to Halstead

Workhouse infirmary, where he died on 4 September of pneumonia brought on by the dunking. Smith and Stammers were brought to court on 8 March 1864, and both were sentenced to six months with hard labour for the assault.

Leechcraft and Cures of Essex Cunning Folk

To cure a sufferer of the ague: go alone to the four cross-ways at night. Just as the clock strikes twelve turn yourself about three times and drive a ten-penny nail into the ground up to the head, and walk away from the place backwards before the clock has finished striking and you'll miss the ague. But the next person to pass over the nail will take it in your stead.

Old Punishments: Transportation

In the early years of the nineteenth century there were almost two hundred offences that carried the death penalty, many of which would today be regarded as relatively minor, such as poaching, sheep stealing and theft. As pressure to abolish hanging increased, transportation became more common in place of the death penalty. Between 1787 and 1868 thousands of male and female British criminals (some under 10 years of age) were transported in prison hulks to Australia. Their crimes varied from three instances of petty theft to rioting. Locked in irons, the prisoners were kept on the ships in appalling conditions until the ships were full and ready to depart on the 252-day journey. As a result, many of the prisoners were weak and malnourished even before the journey started. As many as a quarter of the passengers died before they reached Botany Bay.

One of the last convict ships.

6 August **1616** Will Cooper, 'the dwarf of Giddie Hall', was buried in Romford churchyard on this day. This little man had been retained as part of the entertainments at Gidea Hall for over thirty years. He was so well liked that Richard Cooke, son of the great Sir Anthony, remembered him in his will in 1579: 'To little Will Cooper tenne pounds and 56s 4d by yeare during his life.' Lucky Will stayed at the hall for the rest of his life, enjoying the benefits of this generous bequest.

7 August **1854** George Risby was released from Springfield Gaol. Tried at the Spring Assizes in 1835 for the wilful murder of John Spooner at West Bergholt, Risby was acquitted on the grounds of insanity and was ordered to be detained 'until his Majesty's pleasure be known'. After a lapse of twenty years, due consideration was given to his case and, taking into account his good conduct in prison, the Secretary of State recommended his release.

8 August **1896** Farmer Myhill was wiping the sweat from his brow; his harvest was in full swing and the barn was filling up. Hardly had his men laid up their scythes for the week and prepared to sing 'All is safely gathered in, let the winter storms begin', when the barn at Catmere End was struck by lightning during a freak storm. It was burnt to the ground, causing £420-worth of damage.

9 August **1821** Ruben Collins of Witham, a young man of respectable appearance, was brought before the Essex Summer Assizes. After 'accomplishing the ruin of Hannah Stammers, a servant girl at his father's lodgings', Collins had promised her marriage, but after discovering she was pregnant he sent her a quantity of pennyroyal, accompanied by a letter urging her to take it 'as a remedy for the consequences of their amour'. This had no effect so he gave her some steel pills, and upon their failure he brought her 'electuary', then some twigs she had to boil up and drink, then steel filings, then a phial of red medicine, all of which failed in their desired effect but made the girl very ill. Her parents became involved, and repeatedly demanded that Collins marry the girl; he declined, claiming 'inability' and 'loss of position', so the unhappy girl placed the letters in the hands of Mr Archer, the clerk to the magistrates. Mr Archer duly sent a number of 'reasonable letters' to Collins requesting him to make 'an honest woman' of the girl, but received only offensive rebuttals. Collins was subsequently indicted for wilfully and maliciously administering certain drugs in order to procure an abortion; found guilty, he was sentenced to fourteen years' transportation.

10 August **1775** Lambert Reading was the leader of a desperate gang of hackney coachmen who robbed Copped Hall, the home of the Conyers family, near Epping. Unfortunately one of the gang's coaches was passed by a local magistrate who was surprised to see such a carriage in such a place late at night. When he heard of the burglary the next day, he wrote to Sir John Fielding, a blind police magistrate in London renowned for his team of 'thief-takers', about his concerns. A hue and cry was raised and Fielding's thief-takers traced Reading to a house on Brick Lane, where they also discovered pistols, swords, daggers and diverse items of housebreakers' paraphernalia, including pick-locks and dark lanterns. Lambert came quietly, while the Conyers' goods and plate were recovered from the house in three sacks. After due trial, Lambert kept his appointment with the hangman on this day at Chelmsford.

1882 Newspapers published details of the inquest held at Leyton on the body of Mr E.R. Carr (29), the captain of the Albemarle Cricket Club. During an away match at the Leyton ground, Carr scored a respectable twenty-nine runs before

11 August

he was caught out. As he was retiring to the tent the crowd cheered him for his batting to such a degree it 'excited him and he fell down in a fainting fit'. His colleagues gathered around him and restoratives were administered but he never regained consciousness. After medical evidence was presented at the inquest the jury returned a verdict of 'death from syncope'.

1647 Burial of Matthew Hopkins, Witchfinder-General

12 August

Hopkins originated from the Manningtree area, and worked in the legal office of a shipping company in Ipswich. Although he was described as a lawyer, there is no clear evidence to support this. In 1644 he returned to his family roots at Mistley, where he bought the Thorn Inn. It was in this year that he began to realise there was money to be made from capitalising on local Puritan fears and prejudices by hunting out witches. Often these were simply old, marginal members of rural societies, mostly

Matthew Hopkins,
Witchfinder-General.

vulnerable elderly widows against whom some locals bore a grudge, or perhaps they merely wanted a scapegoat to blame for the untimely loss of a relative or livestock, personal illness, injury or misfortune. Employed by the worthy citizens of towns and villages across East Anglia, Hopkins subsequently sent more witches to the gallows than any other witch-hunter in England and made himself a veritable fortune in the process. Extant and verified records state his efforts were responsible for seventy-four executions for witchcraft and thirty-six deaths in gaol, but the actual figures were probably considerably higher. Folklore likes to tell that Hopkins was suspected of being a witch himself and was punished accordingly – but the truth is he died of a medical condition (now recognised as tuberculosis) and was buried at Mistley on this day.

13 August   **Essex Witches and Witchcraft**
It seems poor 'Dummy' was not the last witch in Sible Hedingham (see 3 August). In 1890 local newspapers reported the story of a man with a horse and cart loaded with straw. As he passed the gate of an old labourer who was supposed to be a wizard, the old man cried out to him, 'You'll not get far with that load.' Brushing the comment aside, the man carried on up the road but within a few feet the horse stumbled and was so badly injured it had to be destroyed. Local men were called to assist with moving the carcass, but on hearing the circumstances they refused to help until a piece of flesh was cut from the horse's hindquarters and burnt. Their reason for this action was well founded in folklore: burning this piece of flesh would cause the person who cast the spell to suffer the same pain on a similar part of their anatomy!

14 August   **1848** Mary May (38) was married and lived with her family at Wix. Her brother William Constable, a pedlar, also lodged with them. One day her brother was working in a nearby field when he was struck down with severe stomach pains and sickness. He did not recover, but little comment was made about his death until it was revealed that Mary had entered her own and her brother's names in a 'burial club' only a short while before he died. William's body was exhumed and the post-mortem revealed enough arsenic in his stomach to kill three strong men. Mary was brought to trial for his murder. The lies she had told when joining the burial club and about her brother's illness came back to haunt her and she was found guilty. She swore she did not commit the murder and amassed great public sympathy, to such an extent that a petition was raised with 1,400 signatures pleading for her death sentence to be commuted to a prison term. However, it failed and Mary was executed by Calcraft at 9.00am on this day on a scaffold erected above the entrance to Chelmsford Gaol before a crowd estimated to have numbered about four thousand people.

15 August   **1888** George Sargeant, a former soldier and one-time poacher of Copford, was employed as a railway labourer. Always a dissolute man, he had resolved

to reform and persuaded his long-suffering girlfriend Annie to marry him at Easter in 1888. But it wasn't long before his violent behaviour drove her out and she went back to live with her parents at Wakes Colne. After several attempts to get her to return, Sargeant arrived at the Wakes Colne residence on 17 July. Amid assurances of good intent and behaviour, he was admitted and allowed to speak to his estranged wife. She, however, was adamant that she would not return home. Flying into a rage, Sargeant pulled her down by the hair, locked her head between his knees and proceeded to cut her throat, despite the terrified screams of her mother and sister. He then ran out of the house but was soon caught hiding in nearby fields. He never denied the crime and was deeply penitent after his conviction. Reports state that he walked firmly to the scaffold at Springfield Gaol; his neck was broken by the 5ft drop, but he still 'struggled rather violently for a few seconds'.

Last Rites

16 August

A few excerpts from the Romford Church burial register:

1612 April 21. Dumb Joan from Holmans, Hare
  Street
1616 Sept. 22. A stranger yt died in ye barn of
  Sir Robert Q. [Sir Robert Quarles of Stewards]
1625 Jan. 11. A woman whom they called madd
  megg
1626 July 18. Toby Asser, killed in a chimney
1657 March 25. Burryed one call'd black John
1657 Aug. 3. Edward Littleton, Knight (Kill'd in a
  duell)

1810 Reports began to be published about a murder case at the Essex Assizes, **17 August** where James Sweeney, Richard Pearce, Edmund Buckley, Patrick Fleming, Maurice Brenwick and John Sullivan were being tried for the murder of John Bolding, the landlord of the Eagle and Child public house at Forest Gate, West Ham. On 20 May a row had erupted in the kitchens between an Irishman named Morrissy and Thomas, a carter. Bolding escorted the aggressive antagonists off the premises and bolted the doors behind them, fearing reprisals. He was right to be concerned. Morrissy returned again later and was admitted, much against Bolding's wishes. Stripped to the waist, Morrissy challenged any man to fight him. Soon afterwards a crowd of about thirty Irish labourers pushed their way in through the door, armed with bludgeons and potato hoes. They believed Bolding had taken Thomas's side in the quarrel and that he had given him shelter in the pub. When a forced search did not reveal the carrier's presence, the mob set about poor John Bolding. Mr Quand, an old man who also lived in the house, tried to escape the violence but was chased and beaten to the ground; three of his teeth were knocked out and his hip dislocated. Sweeney, Pearce, Buckley, Fleming, Brenwick and

Sullivan were all found guilty of being complicit in Bolding's death and were sentenced to death.

18 AUGUST   1891   Thomas Sadler persuaded Mrs Wass to leave her husband and start a new life with him. During an argument with William Wass over custody of the children, Sadler was overcome with rage and stabbed Wass behind the ear with a penknife, killing him instantly. At his trial Sadler remained composed and only broke down after the final meeting with his father and sister. He was executed on this day by James Berry at Springfield Gaol.

19 AUGUST   1810   Reports were circulating about the recent Essex Assizes, where a number of unusual cases had been heard. Thomas Rudd, an old man of 72, was convicted of stealing bark from the estate of Admiral Elijah Harvey at Chigwell and was sentenced to twelve months' imprisonment. Susan Draper, 'a very interesting well-dressed young woman', the daughter of a farmer from Holland in Essex, was charged with stealing a piece of gown cloth from Mr Jarrold's shop at Weeley, valued at 10s. She was found guilty and the judge stated he should really send her for transportation, but in view of her youthfulness he passed a more lenient sentence, in the hope that her confinement would 'be used in reflecting on the very heinous offence she had committed' and would 'induce her to resolve upon a future conduct less disgraceful to herself and friends'. She was then sentenced to the House of Correction for six months. Elizabeth Cox was found guilty of concealing the birth of her child and sentenced to twelve months' confinement in the House of Correction.

20 AUGUST   1805   Thomas Smith, a corporal in the Witham Volunteers, was returning home from exercise when he encountered Joseph Biggs, the proprietor of the Stratford stages, in the company of two women. After several exchanges, Smith dealt a blow to Biggs's head with his musket, which ultimately brought about his death. Mr Taylor the surgeon deposed that Biggs would have recovered from the blow had he not ignored the surgeon's advice to rest. Instead he went to London, where he caught a cold which 'terminated in a locked-jaw, of which he died'. Smith was found not guilty and freed.

21 AUGUST   1856   James Cooper and Egmont and Alfred Hoof, all well-dressed young gentlemen, invited the man they leased stables from, a Brentwood baker, to come and drink with them. He concurred, and bottle after bottle was called for until the poor man was in a helpless state of intoxication. Making a mark across his throat as if it had been cut, and smearing him with copious amounts of ochre, they dumped him in a wheelbarrow and wheeled him down Brentwood High Street to his house. Tragically, the poor man died from congestion of the brain and lungs caused by the large quantity of liquor he had taken. The coroner's jury returned a verdict of death by natural causes, but the magistrates took the prank more seriously and pressed a charge of manslaughter at the Spring Assizes. There was no evidence for malice so the

manslaughter charge was dropped, but the placing of the ochre on the baker constituted a common assault. Found guilty of this crime, the three men were reprimanded for their behaviour by the judge and sentenced to one month in the County Gaol. It was reported that the defendants, 'who evidently had not the least idea that they should undergo imprisonment', appeared 'quite astounded' at the sentence.

Last Rites

22 AUGUST

A unique burial custom was observed in the Soken villages until the early eighteenth century. As a gesture of gratitude, the clergyman who read the burial service over the corpse was offered (or had the right to claim) 'the best upper garment' of the dearly departed.

1906   *The Honeypot Lane Murders.* Albert Watson (47) and his wife Emma (50) were shot and killed while collecting water from a pond on a neighbour's land just off Honey Pot Lane at Basildon. The farmer, Mr Buckham, was happy for the couple to take water from his pond but his sons, Richard (20) and Robert (17), were less keen on the arrangement. Richard Buckham reported the discovery of the bodies to neighbour Mr Stevens,

23 AUGUST

The funeral of Albert and Emma Watson. *(Essex Police Museum)*

Sgt Richard Giggins.
(Essex Police Museum)

and soon Constable Tom Layzell and Police Sergeant Richard Giggins were on the scene. Richard's suspicious behaviour led to closer questioning by Superintendent Alfred Marden, during which Robert alleged that Richard had taken particular offence at the Watsons drawing water from his father's pond. He went on to say that Richard had shot the couple, and had even gone to their house and stolen a watch and some money (4s 6d). Richard admitted he had carried out the shooting in a fit of anger after Mr Watson disrespectfully dismissed his order to get off the land. Richard also admitted taking the watch and the money. Both brothers stood trial for murder. Robert was acquitted but Richard was found guilty and sent to the gallows. He was executed by Henry Pierrepoint at Chelmsford Prison on 4 December 1906.

Old Punishments: Fines for Profanity

Much was made of the laws against profanity in the eighteenth and nineteenth centuries. The fee table used by Essex magistrates under the Profane Oaths Act of 1745 notes the following scale of fines:

For a first offence:

By a day labourer, common soldier, sailor or seaman	1 shilling
By a person under the degree of gentleman	2 shillings
Every person of or above the degree of gentleman	5 shillings

For a second offence the fines were doubled and for a third trebled.

24 August

1856 The mayor and corporation of Harwich were so dissatisfied with their own borough police force that they formally resolved to amalgamate with the county constabulary. Their old chief constable and his men were dismissed on 1 February 1857, and the county force moved in under Inspector Robert Banks. However, unlike the old borough constabulary, the men of this new force were not at the beck and call of the mayor, the committee or the local justices. There were several bitter exchanges between the corporation and Chief Constable McHardy before they realised what it really meant to have county constabulary men policing their town!

25 August

1896 Police became involved in the search for James Taylor (80), a deaf and dumb lunatic who had escaped from Saffron Walden Workhouse infirmary.

26 August

1648 *The end of the Siege of Colchester.* The town and castle surrendered on this day, bringing to an end weeks of misery for the town's starving inhabitants, who were reduced to eating horses, dogs, cats and vermin. On 21 August the women and children of the town were allowed out to seek mercy from Fairfax's men, but they were turned back. On the 27th came news of Cromwell's victory over the Scots. Realising that the Royalist cause was lost, the townsfolk surrendered. Their leaders, Sir Charles Lucas and Sir George Lisle, were taken outside the castle walls and shot on the orders of Sir Thomas Fairfax. Sir Charles faced the firing squad first, declaring bravely, 'See, I am ready for you; and now, rebels, do your worst!' Sir George kissed his

27 August

The Lucas and Lisle memorial near Colchester Castle.

dying friend farewell, and asked the musketeers to come a little closer. One of their number replied, 'I'll warrant ye, sir, we'll hit you.' Sir George smiled and replied, 'I have been nearer you when you missed me.' Rising from his prayers, he cried, 'I am now ready: traitors do your worst.' A memorial to these brave gentlemen now stands on the site of their execution.

28 AUGUST **1819** Leary Brown and Patrick Welsh, two natives of Ireland, attempted to pass a forged Bank of England note at the Fox and Hounds pub in West Ham in payment for a glass of gin. When the men left the pub the note was examined carefully and found to be forged. A servant-girl was sent after them, and they came back with her and returned the change. They then attempted to make their escape but were 'overtaken and secured'. It transpired that Brown and Welsh had previously passed similar notes in Rainham and Avely. Brought before the Assizes, they were found guilty of uttering forged notes and sentenced to death.

29 AUGUST **1746** John Skinner, otherwise known as 'Colchester Jack', was born into a good family at Brightlingsea in 1704. Hopelessly spoilt by his parents, he entered adult life still believing he could have anything he desired. If he could not buy it he would steal it, and if thwarted he would fly into a rage. Despite having a successful business and a wife with a sizeable fortune, he frittered away his money in drinking, gambling and other debauched pleasures. Unable to pay his debts, he took to the lucrative but highly illegal business of smuggling, a business he ran under the cover of two rented farms near Colchester. His partner in crime was Daniel Brett, who concealed his association with Skinner by acting as his servant. On 23 May 1744 Skinner discovered that some contraband he was ready to sell was missing, and Brett was

THE

LIFE *and* BEHAVIOUR

OF

JOHN SKINNER,

Who was Executed *August* 29, 1746, at

CHELMSFORD in *ESSEX*

FOR THE

Murder of DANIEL BRETT,

(his late Servant) the 23d of *May*, 1744.

CONTAINING

I. A true Account of his Birth, Family, Education, and being put Apprentice to an eminent Oilman near St. Andrew's Church in Holborn.

II. His Marriage to a young Lady of good Family and Fortune in Essex, and setting up for himself without Aldgate; with the gay Manner in which he liv'd.

III. His cruel Usage to his Wife, whose Company he deserted for the Sake of Town-Ladies, so that she was obliged to go into the Parish Workhouse.

IV. His becoming a Bankrupt, and retiring to Rum-ford, where he kept an Inn, and afterwards commenc'd Smuggler.

V. His shooting his Servant, for which he fled; his being apprehended; Commitment; Copies of the Affidavits made relating to the Murder; and his Trial at the Bar.

VI. His Deportment under Condemnation; a Letter to his Friend; and how he stabb'd himself the Morning of his Execution, to avoid a shameful Death.

VII. His Advice to all the Smugglers; his Behaviour and dying Words at the Place of Execution.

LONDON:

Printed for J. Thompson, Publisher, near the Sessions-House in the Old-Baily; and may be had at the Pamplet-shops and of the News-sellers. [Price Three-pence.]

responsible for it. Flying into one of his rages, he declared he would 'shoot him [Brett] as dead as a carrion crow, and then let him go and ask pardon of God Almighty'. He searched for him for several hours, and when he finally found him he was still furious – and shot him, just as he had threatened. Immediately regretting his actions, Skinner was relieved to find he had only wounded Brett, who was taken to a place of safety. Unfortunately he died a few hours later. Skinner disappeared until 1746, when a minor property deal brought him out of hiding to complete the paperwork. He was arrested and brought to trial. Found guilty of the murder, he was sentenced to death and executed at Chelmsford on this day.

1914 *Russian Troops in Essex?* Within weeks of the country's mobilisation for war, troops in transit to foreign service or home defence positions had become a familiar sight, especially in coastal areas and on the railways. Rumours of exotic troops, specifically Russians, 'still with snow on their boots', being spotted on stations in Essex were circulating widely at this time. One rumour recorded by the Revd Andrew Clark of Great Leighs said that Russian troops from Archangel had landed in Scotland and were being hurriedly driven south on commandeered East Coast trains to take their place in the theatre of war in Belgium. They were apparently fed during a stop-off in Colchester. However, there was no substance to these rumours – there were no Russian troops either passing through or stationed in Britain in 1914.

30 August

German prisoners arriving at Southend, 1917. They were housed in derelict ship hulks just off shore.

31 August **Leechcraft and Cures of Essex Cunning Folk**

A certain charm to cure toothache could be obtained from an ancient inhabitant of Brent Pelham. It consisted of something believed to be the leg of a frog or toad sewn in a little bag, to be worn next to the skin.

The trial of the 'Siege Captains' Sir Charles Lucas and Sir George Lisle restaged at Colchester Pageant.

SEPTEMBER

The funeral cortège of Dr Barnardo, 1905. The tireless efforts of Dr Thomas John Barnardo, the founder of the children's homes, drove him to sickness and an early grave. He died on 19 September 1905, aged just 60. It was his wish that his body should be cremated and then buried in the grounds of his 'Village Home' at Barkingside. More than 1,500 children from every branch of the homes, along with staff, friends and well-wishers, accompanied him on his last sad journey.

1 SEPTEMBER **1905** The first major train crash of the twentieth century took place on this day in Essex. The Cromer Express was packed with passengers looking forward to their holidays in the 'Poppyland' of the north Norfolk coast, but as it swept through Witham station, travelling at a speed estimated to have been somewhere between 50 and 70mph, the train left the rails, causing its fourteen carriages to break apart. Some of the central carriages overturned and smashed onto the platform. In all, ten people, including Josiah Doole the station porter, were killed and another sixty injured. Luckily the train coming through the station in the opposite direction was a couple of minutes late and was stopped in time to prevent further carnage. After a long inquiry the blame was attributed to a group of platelayers who had been working on the line just minutes before the train came through; they had failed to tighten sufficiently one of the keys that held the rail in place.

The Cromer Express disaster, Witham, 1905.

2 SEPTEMBER **1845** An inquest was held on this day at Springfield Gaol into the death of William Blackburn. He and his wife worked as servants at Stondon Hall. The body of Mrs Blackburn was found lying on the bed with her throat cut, but her husband was nowhere to be seen. Later in the day he was discovered in a nearby wood with a frightful wound to his throat. A razor was found in his pocket, and he admitted killing his wife and inflicting his own wound. Too ill to stand trial at the Assizes, he was held at Springfield under constant supervision and kept alive with 'nutritive injections'. The inquest agreed he eventually died from extreme exhaustion and the wounds 'inflicted by himself whilst in a state of temporary insanity'.

1878 The *Princess Alice* was one of the most popular pleasure-steamers on the Thames. Returning from Sheerness on the evening of 3 September 1878, she was loaded to the gunnels with day-tripping Londoners. (In fact she was heavily overloaded: her official capacity was 500, but on this occasion she was carrying about 700 passengers.) As the steamer entered the stretch of river near Barking Creek, the ironclad collier *Bywell Castle* (a vessel five times heavier than the *Princess Alice*) was also on the water, en route to Newcastle. For some reason Captain Grinstead of the steamer suddenly changed course, and the *Bywell Castle* could not avoid her. The collier's bows struck just forward of the starboard paddle-box, almost cutting the *Princess Alice* in two. She sank in less than four minutes. More than 640 people drowned, but many bodies were never recovered. The Thames-side towns of Rainham, East Ham and Barking were deeply affected by the disaster and a subscription was raised for the bereaved. In the days afterwards the waters around Woolwich were filled with dozens of small vessels as enterprising folk sought to recover the bodies: each carcass earned its finder the princely sum of 12 shillings. Many unseemly struggles and fights ensued over the bodies of the dead.

3 September

1914 As thousands of young men volunteered for war service all across the country, the patriotic fervour of the civilian population saw many outbursts of violence against anything German. 'Aliens' were rounded up and incarcerated under the Defence of the Realm Act, businesses with German-sounding names had their windows smashed, German products from clocks to toys were purged, smashed or burnt, and people with German-sounding names were treated with great suspicion. (It was at this time that the royal family, itself of German descent, changed its name from Saxe-Coburg-Gotha to Windsor.) The general mood led to many spy scares. For example, stories circulated around Mistley and neighbouring parishes that a spy had approached the Tendring Hundred waterworks (near the railway station) and flashed an electric light. The military sentries challenged the man but he ran off amid a volley of rifle fire and disappeared into a wood. Another rumour told how one of the sentries on guard at the Marconi station in Chelmsford was shot in a drive-by shooting 'by German agents in a motor'.

4 September

1896 The community of Pebmarsh was just beginning to come to terms with the shocking murder committed just a few days earlier by local farmer Samuel Collis. Few locals knew that Collis had once been committed to a private lunatic asylum, and he had lived peaceably in the locality for a number of years. The trouble began when he decided not to go to bed but stayed up all night roaming around his widowed mother's farm on stilts. At 5.45am Mrs Turpin, one of Collis's married sisters, came into the yard to let the fowls out. Collis approached, knocked her down and declared he was 'going to clear the lot off'. Mrs Turpin got up and ran to the house where she and her mother barred the doors. Collis was infuriated by this and began

5 September

smashing the windows with the butt of his gun. John Cockerill, the farm bailiff, soon arrived on the scene and told Collis to go away. His demand was met with a blast from the shotgun. Local policeman Harry Cook arrived at about 6.00am and met Collis coming out of the field with some dead poultry under his arm. He said to the constable, 'I have killed a sheep and here is the head' – and with those words he handed a basin to Cook, who was horrified to find it contained the severed head of the farm bailiff! Collis then leapt over the wall in an attempt to escape but PC Cook bravely pursued him. Even when Collis drew his revolver, Cook would not back off; instead he drew his truncheon and threatened to use it. Eventually the two men clashed, and Cook threw Collis to the ground and took possession of the gun. He also found on him a bloodstained carving knife. With some assistance, the courageous constable managed to get Collis into custody.

6 SEPTEMBER   **Essex beliefs and omens that warn of the approach of the Angel of Death**

If a swarm of bees alights either on a dead tree or on a dead bough of a living tree near the house, there will be a death in the family in the near future. In Essex the tradition of 'telling the bees' about a death in the family was a well-observed custom for it was believed the bees would take such offence they would desert their hives if they were not kept informed. The nineteenth-century ceremony was recorded in a parish near Colchester: 'A procession was formed up for the formal announcement to the bees, and sundry pieces of black cloth and the key to the main door of the house were taken to the hives. A piece of black cloth was solemnly bound around each hive, given three taps with the key and the bees informed their master was dead.'

7 SEPTEMBER   **1940** On this day the 'Cromwell' codeword (which indicated an imminent German invasion) was given out in error, and there were dozens of scares all across the country. From this date rumours began to circulate about large numbers of dead bodies washed ashore along the south-east coast; these were thought to be German troops from the thwarted invasion force who had been severely burnt by oil bombs and flame barrages. Hundreds of bodies were said to have been found on the beach at Clacton, while it was even whispered that the numbers of bodies washed up on the beach at Southend were so great that the remains were collected in corporation dustcarts. Flame barrages had indeed been tested off the coast of Essex, and this doubtless lay at the bottom of most of these rumours. But they were not entirely fictional. A number of ordinary people with no motive to lie swore they saw numerous unexplained bodies washed up on the beaches of the east coast in September 1940. Were the bodies actually those of British servicemen washed up after a training exercise went horribly wrong? Or was it all just black propaganda intended to alarm any potential invader and

County Borough of Southend-on-Sea.

AIR RAID PRECAUTIONS.

GENERAL INFORMATION AND ADVICE

TO THE PUBLIC.

AIR RAID WARNINGS AND SIGNALS.

(1) **Warning of an impending Air Raid** will be given by a **Fluctuating** or **Warbling Signal** of varying pitch or by a succession of **intermittent blasts** by hooters and syrens. The police and Air Raid Wardens may repeat the warning by blowing **whistles in short blasts.**

(2) If **Poison Gas** has been used, warning will be given by **Hand Rattles** whilst the ringing of **Hand Bells** will announce that the danger from gas has passed.

(3) The " **Raiders Passed** " Signal will be a **continuous signal of steady pitch.**

ACTION to be taken on hearing warning of impend-

ing Air Raid :—

(1) If at home, go at once to the refuge room which you have provided in your house, or go to the shelter trench in your garden, if you have one. Take your gas mask with you and at once put it on if gas is present.

(2) DO NOT GO OUT INTO THE STREET.

(3) If you are away from your home, go at once to the nearest Public Air Raid Shelter or to one of the Public Trenches which have been provided. These are only intended for persons who happen to be away from their homes when the Air Raid Warning is given ; IF YOU ARE AT HOME, STAY THERE.

Air-raid precautions for Southend, 1940.

reassure the British public in their 'darkest hour' about the strength of Britain's anti-invasion defences?

1913 On this day Constable Joseph Watt of Essex Police died in Romford Cottage Hospital from injuries received while attempting to stop a runaway carthorse, which had been startled by a motor car. As the horse bolted, Watt managed to seize hold of it, but it had lost its bridle and he was unable to control it. He clung on grimly for some distance before he stumbled and was thrown violently to the ground; the wheels of the cart passed over his body, causing the fatal injuries.

8 September

1909 The Great Eastern Stores, owned by Messrs W.A. Wilson & Co., was found to be on fire at 6.00am. The stores dominated a prominent road junction still known as Wilson's Corner in Brentwood and consisted of seven departments offering all manner of goods for the home, from hardware to furnishings. The fire had started in the cellars where the paint, oils and other highly flammable products were stored, and was thought to

9 September

Wilson's fire, Brentwood, 1909.

have been caused by a spark. Several firecrews came from the town and district, and hundreds of onlookers gathered to watch the spectacle. Much criticism was levelled at the inadequacy of the water supply from the local water company. Damages were estimated in the region of £20,000.

10 SEPTEMBER

Leechcraft and Cures of Essex Cunning Folk

To cure wens or fleshy excrescences, pass the hand of a dead body over the part affected on three successive days. The hand of a suicide or executed murderer was deemed more efficacious than that of a person who died a natural death. In the days of public executions a hangman could occasionally be bribed to allow a sufferer onto the scaffold to enable the wen to be stroked by the hand of the executed felon while he still swung on the rope. This behaviour was deeply resented by the crowd, who would boo and jeer at the proceedings.

The efficacious touch of the executed felon.

1841 Essex police constables Robert Pack and Robert Adams appeared in full uniform in the dock at Colchester magistrates court on this day. An account was presented of how the two constables had been out drinking, and wanted to carry on their revelries into the small hours at what they thought was a party being held at the home of Mrs Elizabeth Warren in Wivenhoe. Arriving at her door quite drunk, they were refused admission and a row erupted which ended up with Pack forcing his way past Mrs Warren. He was later charged with assault for this, while Adams was brought up for being drunk. Chief Constable McHardy was in court to see Pack sent down for one month's hard labour, and he assured the justices that even if they discharged Adams without penalty he would be dismissed from the force.

11 SEPTEMBER

1690 The infamous Essex highwayman Frank Osborne (29) was executed at Tyburn on this day. Born to wealthy parents at Colchester in 1661, Osborne was apprenticed to a goldsmith on Lombard Street in London and then set up his own business. Unfortunately he took to gambling and lost so much money that his business suffered and he could not pay his debts. Rather than suffer the ignominy of being sent to a debtors' prison, he set about stealing to pay off his debts – and living well to boot – as a gentleman of the road. His most daring coup occurred on the Harwich–Manningtree road, where he and a companion held up the Earl of Albemarle's coach. The coach was defended by armed outriders and coachmen but all proved to be poor shots and failed to hit the two highwaymen. The earl had no option but to hand over his purse containing 130 guineas, a gold watch and all his jewellery. Osborne was finally brought to book when he and his companions tried to hold up a coach on Hounslow Heath. This time they were outgunned and his companions fled, leaving him surrounded. With no option but to surrender, Osborne was incarcerated in Newgate Prison. At his trial he was sentenced to death for highway robbery and ended up as a 'gallows apple on the Tyburn tree'.

12 SEPTEMBER

1665 The famous diarist Samuel Pepys visited the home of Sir W. Hickes at Leyton and recorded his visit thus: 'It is a good seat, with a fair grove of trees by it, and the remains of a good garden; but so let run to ruin, both house and everything in and about it, so ill-furnished and miserably looked after, [he had] not so much as a latch to his dining-room door. . . . He did give us the meanest dinner, of beef, shoulder and umbles of venison, which he takes away from the keeper of the forest, and a few pigeons, and all in the meanest manner that I ever did see, to the basest degree.'

13 SEPTEMBER

14 SEPTEMBER   **County Gaols and Bridewells of Essex visited by Prison Reformer John Howard**
Barking Bridewell was visited in 1776, 1779 and 1782. It was described as having one room for men, the 'fore-gaol' measuring 15ft by 10½ft and 7ft high, with two windows that looked onto the street. Another room, the 'back-gaol', was for women. This measured 13ft 4in by 11ft and stood 8ft high, with just one window about 2ft square. The rooms were planked all over and had no chimneys, and both rooms were 'made offensive by sewers in them'. There was no court for fresh air but the keeper had a large garden. No water was accessible to the prisoners; they were given an allowance of 3d a day for food but were given no employment to occupy them. On his visit in 1779 Howard found the bridewell occupied by only one prisoner, who shared his space with five men who had been caught by the press-gang and were awaiting collection by the military.

15 SEPTEMBER   **Essex Witches and Witchcraft**
In 1861 a charge of witchcraft was brought against Mrs Legitten at Castle Hedingham. A search of her house had revealed a quantity of brimstone, red ochre and other 'trappings of the blackest arts', which were all presented in court, but the magistrates brushed the matter aside and proceeded with more conventional hearings.

16 SEPTEMBER   **1897**   The Revd F.A. Adams of Doddinghurst Rectory, Brentwood, announced the closure of the Essex Storm Relief Fund. On 30 June a 'terrible visitation' of hail lasting just fifteen minutes had caused fearful damage to buildings and destroyed the corn harvest from over 15,000 acres of land. Great national and local press coverage generated widespread sympathy and a sum approaching £50,000 was raised, enabling a payment of £4 an acre in compensation to the most needy cases.

17 SEPTEMBER   **Leechcraft and Cures of Essex Cunning Folk**
If several children are ill with the whooping cough, take some of the hair of the eldest child, cut it into small pieces, put them into some milk and give the mixture to the youngest child to drink and so on through the family.

Other popular cures from the Suffolk/Essex borders were to let the patient eat a mouse or drink some milk that a ferret has lapped, or to let the patient be dragged under a gooseberry bush or bramble, both ends of which had to be growing in the ground.

18 SEPTEMBER   **1904**   Between 6 and 20 September a large-scale mock invasion was staged at strategic positions along the Essex coast. Britain had not suffered an actual invasion since the Norman Conquest of 1066 but there had been numerous scares in the interim, notably in 1588 when the Spanish Armada sailed past and again during the Napoleonic Wars. During the nineteenth century Britain fought most of her wars in far-flung corners of the Empire, so an 'invasion' staged here drew not only military observers but also

great numbers of the civilian population who came to watch the spectacle. For the first time mechanical lorries and motorcycles were used in the exercise, and the army was soon to find out what happened if a staff car or motorcycle got a good dunking in salt-water!

Landing troops for the mock invasion of Essex, 1904.

19 September

1871 James Bass Mullinger, a Cambridge graduate of 'some literary distinction', visited Annie Haslam, his stepbrother's wife, who was staying with a relative, Mrs Barnard, at Harlow. During the visit Mullinger appeared to be seized with some mania: he took up a knife from the supper table and struck Annie Haslam on the left side. Fortunately the knife was old and worn and Mrs Haslam's dress was so well padded that the knife did not penetrate, but such was the force of the blow that it broke the blade. Undeterred, Mullinger picked up another knife and delivered some eighteen wounds to her throat, face and hands before Mrs Haslam could get away with Mrs Barnard. Mullinger was then seen to calmly pick up his hat and coat and walk back to his father's house, also in Harlow. The police were summoned, and luckily, over the following weeks, Mrs Haslam recovered from her wounds. The case was brought before the Winter Assizes. A number of witnesses spoke favourably of Mullinger's academic prowess, and Dr Bateson, Master of St John's College, stated that he had won a number of prizes, including the Le Bas and Hulsean essays. In an appeal to the jury his defence counsel argued that Mullinger's lameness had greatly soured his temper; this, combined with his devotion to study and literary work, caused a temporary mania to manifest itself on the fateful evening. Mrs Haslam pointed out she had no vindictive feelings towards the prisoner and that a lesser charge than attempted murder would be preferable. A verdict of unlawful wounding was returned and Mullinger was sentenced to twelve months without hard labour.

20 SEPTEMBER 1887 Chelmsford residents were shocked to read about a terrible accident. A horse drawing a two-wheeled trap driven by Essex Chief Constable, Major William Henry Poyntz had bolted across the High Street towards the coaching entrance to the Saracen's Head Hotel. His passenger Colonel Cobbe, a government inspector, was thrown from the vehicle and knocked unconscious. A few yards further on the careering horse and trap smashed into an elderly lady, Mrs Garmeson, and her young relative, Miss Remnant. Miss Remnant was dragged into the yard where the horse only stopped when it crashed into another vehicle parked there. Miss Remnant suffered injuries to her legs and spent the week at the hotel recovering, as did Colonel Cobbe. Sadly Mrs Garmeson had suffered such severe head injuries that she died an hour later, despite receiving immediate medical attention. At the inquest a verdict of accidental death was recorded. Poor Major Poyntz never recovered, and his letter of resignation was received by the County Justices on 2 March 1888.

Essex Chief Constable, William Henry Poyntz.

21 SEPTEMBER 1574 Thomas Reed, Simon Jones and Rise Laugher were executed near Romford Common for stealing soldiers' money. The gallows from which they (and many others) were hanged stood in an area known for generations afterwards as Gallows Field.

22 SEPTEMBER **Essex Witches and Witchcraft**
A carter was driving his wagon up Bread and Cheese Hill in Thundersley when he overtook 'a wisen old crone' who was toiling up the hill with her boot-lace trailing on the ground. The carter called out to warn her, and almost immediately a wheel came off his wagon, went rolling down the hill and toppled over at the bottom. Jumping off the wagon, the carter ran

down the hill and when he got to the wheel he began to flog it unmercifully with his whip. Upon this, the old woman cried out in mortal pain, imploring him to stop the whipping!

Old Punishments: The Pillory

The pillory was an effective and humiliating punishment for seditious speech and sexual crimes dating back to the statutes of the thirteenth century. In England pillories were considered so essential by the authorities that towns which failed to maintain one risked forfeiting the right to hold a market. In Essex the pillories seem to have been particularly pertinent as there were numerous cases of fraudulent traders who had diluted milk, mixed shavings with oats or used 'doctored' weights and measures and were sentenced to 'stand' in the market-place pillory on market day. Here the miscreant would be jeered at and pelted with rotten fruit and vegetables, mud, excrement and even dead animals, depending on their offence and the mood of the crowd. The last man pilloried in England was Peter Bossy, who was found to have lied under oath; his punishment was carried out on Tower Hill, London, on 22 June 1832.

23 September

1916 Zeppelin L33 was returning over Essex after bombing London when it was intercepted by a squadron of night-fighters from Hainault Farm. The airship was badly damaged in the attack and Kapitan Alois Bocker

24 September

Mrs Lewis and her family; their cottage at Little Wigborough was narrowly missed by the crashing Zeppelin.

knew he could not get back to his base. He decided to make a forced landing near New Hall Cottages at Little Wigborough. Warning the cottagers to stand back, he set fire to the airship and then formed up his crew into an orderly body and marched them off towards Peldon. Having seen the ball of flames, Special Constable Edgar Nicholas was hurrying towards the scene on his bicycle. As he came upon the German soldiers in the darkness, Bocker asked him, in good English, how many miles it was to Colchester. Nicholas replied 'about six', and then went on toward the fire and the soldiers marched on. Nicholas had detected Bocker's German accent; worried he would be overpowered and possibly killed, he followed the men at a discreet distance. As they approached Peldon they were met by Special Constable Elijah Taylor and Sergeant Ernest Edwards, who escorted the Germans to Peldon post office, where they found PC Charles Smith. He formally arrested the German crew. Joined by other special constables, the brave PC Smith led the way to Mersea Island, where the Germans could be handed over to the military. En route, however, they encountered a military detachment and the captured crew were handed over. PC Smith's cool head and quick thinking were rewarded by his promotion to sergeant and he was awarded a merit badge. Known from that day forward as 'Zepp' Smith, he retired from the force in 1924 and died in 1977 at the grand old age of 94.

25 SEPTEMBER

The Witchfinder-General: Swimming a Witch

Matthew Hopkins encouraged the swimming of suspected witches but wrote that he never presented evidence based on it. 'Swimming' was one of the most basic (and public) methods of ascertaining 'proof' of a person being a witch or not. Stripped to an undershift, the suspected witch would be 'cross-bound' left thumb to right big toe and right thumb to left big toe and thrown publicly into the nearest dirty village pond or stagnant ditch. They were given three 'dips'; if they sank and drowned they were deemed inno-

'Swimming' a witch.

cent and thus eligible for Christian burial. Those who floated and survived the ordeal could face imprisonment, torture to reveal any others complicit in their diabolical actions, and eventual execution by hanging or burning. Many years after Hopkins's death, the Coggeshall parish register of 1699 records the death of Widow Common, who 'was counted a witch' and was put in the river to see if she would sink. This cruel treatment of an old lady undoubtedly resulted in her untimely demise; sadly, she was not to be last person to suffer this treatment in Essex!

26 SEPTEMBER

1449 A Canterbury manuscript records in precise detail an account of a fight between two dragons at Little Cornard. When the great roars of unknown beasts were heard in the village a few of the bravest local men armed with staffs and spears went to investigate. Arriving at the scene, they were aghast to see two great dragons fighting; one was red and moved on legs, while the other was black and lacked legs, moving instead by a kind of slithering roll. Twisting around the field, the dragons lunged and clawed at each other. One even breathed fire for over an hour. Both were wounded and neither was able to gain the upper hand, so they went their separate ways: the red dragon sloped off to Ballingdon Hill in Essex, south of the Stour, while the black one slithered back to Kedlington Hill.

27 SEPTEMBER

1927 On this day PC George William Gutteridge was shot and killed in the line of duty. George Gutteridge had joined the Essex Constabulary in 1910.

The lane where PC Gutteridge was shot.

After military service in the First World War he rejoined the police in 1919 and became the village bobby at Stapleford Abbotts in 1922. In the early hours of 27 September 1922 he stopped a motor car (later discovered to be stolen) to enquire into the business of the occupants at such an early time. His polite enquiries were met with two shots from a revolver. Mortally wounded, he fell to the ground but the gunman wasn't finished yet; he got out of the car and shot him twice more, once through each eye. As the news broke in the national press the country was horrified by this callous murder. Police enquiries soon led them to the garage of Frederick Guy Browne, and when his premises were searched two Webley revolvers were discovered. William Henry Kennedy, who until recently had been living in the back room of the garage, was traced and arrested in Liverpool. He gave a statement in which he admitted helping steal the car and being in it when Browne shot PC Gutteridge. Browne swore it was Kennedy who stole the car and shot the policeman, and claimed that he had been at home with his wife. In one of the first cases in which ballistics played a key role

PC George Gutteridge. *(Essex Police Museum)*

Frederick Guy
Browne and William
Henry Kennedy.

in the case, it was proved that the pistols found in the garage had fired the fatal shots. Browne and Kennedy were both found guilty and sentenced to death. They were dispatched by executioners Robert Baxter and Thomas Pierrepoint at Pentonville and Wandsworth respectively on 31 May 1928.

Leechcraft and Cures of Essex Cunning Folk

28 SEPTEMBER

To charm away warts and sores, count them, then take a black snail and stick it on a thorn bush; as the snail perishes the blemishes will disappear, provided the sufferer did not tell a soul what they had done.

Essex Witches and Witchcraft

29 SEPTEMBER

If a witch looked in at a window dire consequences could be suffered by the people inside if they met her glance. To protect the household against the power of the witch's glance, it was customary to keep flowers such as St John's wort on the window-sill. One account heard round many an Essex fireside told the story of a woman who did not heed the advice of her superstitious neighbours and refused to buy a broom from a witch who was selling them at the door. Sent away 'with a flea in her ear', the witch stole round the back of the house and peered in at the window. A young boy looked up and met her glance and 'from that day onwards the boy's mind was turned'.

1817 The final dastardly deed of the Elsingham Gang was committed on this day. They had already perpetrated several robberies and burglaries in the county and were the terror of their neighbourhood. On this night the gang of Miller, Giffin, William and James Clarke met at the Clarke residence in Hanly where they blacked their faces and set out to break into the home of James Dennis at Elsingham. Hearing the noise of the parlour window being forced, Mr Dennis rose and challenged the intruders, calling out 'Who's there?' The reply came, 'Damn you, old buffer, we'll let you know.' Dennis had asked his maid to bring him a light and he

30 SEPTEMBER

was going to investigate when two shots rang through the shutter of the window being assaulted. Mr Dennis was wounded under the eye and near the nose. A man named James Pearce came running up to enquire into the commotion, and was told to hold his tongue or he should fare worse. He thought it prudent to retire. When the gang returned to the Clarke house Mrs Clarke advised them to bury their pistol and dark lantern in the adjoining orchard. The local constable soon pulled together the witnesses and recovered the lantern and pistol. Brought to justice at the next Assizes, the judge ensured that lengthy terms of imprisonment for some and death sentences for others would put an end to the notorious Elsingham Gang.

OCTOBER

The north door of the church in the charming village of Hadstock is Saxon and is claimed to be the oldest door still in use in the country. Local folklore tells that the skin of a Dane found guilty of theft was nailed to the door as a warning to others. The tale gained a disturbing degree of credence when a piece of skin was found in the door during repairs. It has been analysed and confirmed as human; it belonged to a fair-haired man who was going grey and was dated to about the eleventh century.

1 OCTOBER **1862** *Captain McGorrery's Tragedies.* Captain McGorrery was the Governor of Springfield Gaol in Chelmsford from 1861 to 1881. Shortly after he and his family moved into the governor's residence within the prison walls his 7-year-old son William died of diphtheria on 2 August 1862. A week after his death his sister Ann contracted the same illness and died on 15 August. Tragically, any outbreak of a contagious disease in the prison was just as likely to spread to the governor's house as to any other part of the prison. After Ann's death the family moved out for a month, while the house was newly whitewashed throughout and 'due precautions taken' to rid the house of any infestations and infections. It served for naught. A fortnight after their return their 5-year-old daughter Mary Ann contracted scarlet fever and died on 1 October. The family then vacated the house permanently.

2 OCTOBER **1922** At about midnight Percy Thompson (34) and his wife Edith (32) were walking back to their home at 41 Kensington Gardens, Ilford, after an evening at the theatre when a man wearing an overcoat rushed up to them. He pushed Edith away and challenged Percy; the ensuing argument rapidly erupted into a fight during which Percy was fatally stabbed. Edith recognised the overcoat as one belonging to a man named Frederick Bywaters (21). The police investigation soon revealed that Bywaters and Edith Thompson had been having an affair, and both were arrested on 4 October, Bywaters claiming he knew nothing about the murder and Edith moaning 'Oh God, why did he do it?' Soon the love-letters that Edith had regularly sent to Bywaters when he was away at sea came to light. These letters contained newspaper cuttings from current murder trials and vague notions of killing Percy – plans that were made much of at the ensuing trial. Bywaters's guilt was never really in doubt but the question of whether Edith really had plotted with the infatuated young man to murder her husband remains unproven. Nevertheless, Thompson and Bywaters were both hanged on the morning of 9 January 1923 at Holloway prison.

3 OCTOBER **1900** William Burrett (35) was an unemployed hawker, whose wife Ada had turned to prostitution in desperation. On the morning of 25 August 1900 Ada informed her husband that she was not going to support him any longer with her immoral earnings. Flying into a rage, Burrett stabbed Ada no fewer than nine times. Help soon arrived at their Alexandra Street home in Plaistow and Ada was taken to hospital, but she died of her wounds later that evening. Burrett appeared at the Old Bailey charged with murder, and so overwhelming was the evidence against him that the trial lasted only one day. He was executed on this day at Chelmsford by James Billington.

4 OCTOBER **Essex Witches and Witchcraft**
In October 1944 the headlines of the *Sunday Pictorial* proclaimed 'Witch Walks at Scrapfaggot Green'. A certain Agnes Haven, found guilty of witchcraft at Chelmsford Assizes in 1593, had allegedly been brought back to Scrapfaggot Green and burnt at the stake there. A great stone was then

placed over her ashes to prevent her ghost from walking. In 1943, when American servicemen widened the road for their air base construction vehicles, they unceremoniously heaved the stone into a ditch – and it was then that strange things began to occur. Sheep strayed from secure fields, church bells rang at ungodly hours and geese disappeared. Later accounts claimed that up to thirty sheep and two horses had inexplicably died, the church clock ran backwards, hens stopped laying and cows aborted. Serious investigation has revealed little evidence for the whole story, and it seems that no witches were ever burnt in Essex . . . but as the old saying goes, there's no smoke without fire!

Grim Tales of Essex   5 October

There was said to be a haunted tree in Barling. From one of the mighty branches a baker, overwhelmed by some personal tragedy, had hanged himself, but his spirit never left the tree. Numerous stories were told about the tree to frighten local children. Among the tales it was said that on windy nights you could quite distinctly hear his ghostly heels knocking together as he swung from the branch. Another said that if you ran a hundred times around the tree you would see the phantom baker making bread. A local wag drew an audience as he attempted the feat, but he slipped and sprained his ankle on the 99th circuit – a salutary lesson to the unwary not to tinker with the spirit world!

1863 Mary Ann Bastard, a servant-girl at the residence of William White   6 October
in Stansted Mountfitchett, came downstairs at 7.00am and discovered the secretaire had been forced open and the contents strewn about. After further investigation of other rooms it soon became apparent the house had been broken into. Mary ran upstairs to warn her master. Mr White pulled on a few clothes and came down with her. Looking around the lower part of the house he found the cellar door open, and suspected the thief might still be down there. He sent Mary for a light and they began to descend the stairs. Suddenly a pistol shot rang out from the darkness, narrowly missing Mary. Mr White hurried to the outside door and shouted 'Murder!' The man in the cellar then bolted out into the back garden, but found he had no escape route. Neighbours

ran out to see what was happening and saw the intruder point his pistol at Mr White. Keeping his concerned neighbours well back, White decided to confront the man, armed with a shotgun brought by one of the neighbours. When he pointed the shotgun at the man, he called out 'Oh, fair play', threw his pistol on the lawn and surrendered. The constable was soon on the scene and the man, who gave his name as Clement Fletcher, was taken into custody.

7 OCTOBER **Old Punishments: The Treadmill**

The treadmill was devised in the early nineteenth century by the Suffolk engineer and iron founder William Cubitt. The principle of the original treadmill was simple. It looked like an elongated mill wheel, some 16ft in diameter, containing on the inside twenty-four steps set 8in apart. As the convicts 'walked' up the steps, the wheel revolved, typically twice a minute; a mechanism rang a bell on every thirtieth revolution to announce the end of the spell of work. Every man put to labour at the wheel worked fifteen quarter-hour sessions a day, climbing up to 18,000ft every day. In Springfield Gaol there were eight treadmills, each 5ft in diameter, but varying in length from 9½ to 26ft. The number usually employed at this labour in the gaol was between twelve and twenty. Those unable to walk the treadmill were obliged to push capstans round instead. Both these devices were connected to pumps which supplied water for the use of the prisoners and cleansed their sewers. In 1895 there were thirty-nine treadmills and twenty-nine cranks in use in British prisons. Treadmills were finally banned by an Act of Parliament in 1898.

8 OCTOBER 1812 The Post Office Packet *Lady Frances* came alongside on Harwich river and was routinely boarded by Mr Haggis, an officer of the customs. On searching the vessel Haggis found a quantity of tea and spirits that had been hidden away by the crew, and announced that it was his duty to seize the vessel in the name of the king. The captain and master of the packet, J.W. Butter, was on shore at the time and was immediately sent for. On his return, Butter and Haggis went below decks to discuss the matter in the captain's cabin. Informing him of the situation, Haggis advised him to apply to shore for relief. Under a Parliamentary Act men accused of smuggling were to be sent to a man-of-war to be detained. When the two men came up on deck, they were alarmed to see most of the crew rowing away in a small boat. The captain called for his gun, loaded it with ball cartridge and then told the escaping crew to return or he would shoot. Raising the gun to his side, rather than to his shoulder, Butter fired, but thought the shot had passed over the boat. He reloaded, but this time Haggis took the gun and fired it into the air. Both believed no mischief had been done, but it turned out that Seaman John Farr had been shot dead. At the trial in March 1812 the defence argued that the killing was 'justifiable homicide' because the crew were under martial law. Testimonials were given about Captain Butter, and it was pointed out that he had supported Farr's family since the tragic event. The jury passed a verdict of manslaughter, and Butter was sentenced to pay a fine of 1s, after which he was discharged.

Essex Witches and Witchcraft

In 1857 the vicar of East Thorpe was compelled to mount guard in person over the door of a suspected witch in the village to avoid the poor old woman being dragged out of her home and 'swum' in the village pond.

Grim Tales of Essex

Sometime in the seventeenth century Lord Campden the Lord Chief Justice was walking through Stifford with Lord Dacres. As they passed the stocks Campden asked if he might try them to see what it felt like to be in the stocks. He sat down and inserted his feet, and Dacres locked down the bar – and then rode off towards Aveley, leaving poor Campden in the stocks. Released a little later, Campden took the prank in good humour but he never forgot the experience. When a question arose in court concerning punishment by the stocks, his lordship was able to tell counsel, with feeling, 'I've tried them, brother, and they are not pleasant.'

1933 On Friday 7 July 1933 Robert James Kirby (26) went to visit the family

of his girlfriend, Grace Newing (17), at 28 Stevens Road, Chadwell Heath. She was expected home after work at 11.30pm and he spent the evening playing with her young brother, who was amusing himself with a piece of cord, and chatting to her mother. Mrs Newing went to bed at 10.45pm, leaving Kirby alone downstairs. She heard Grace come in, and shortly after there was a commotion downstairs; going down to investigate, Mrs Newing found Grace dead on the floor, strangled with the cord her brother had been playing with earlier that evening. Kirby was nowhere to be seen. He had fled to his family home and confessed. His brother fetched a policeman, and took him to the murder scene. Meanwhile, Kirby went to his brother's house on Westdown Road, where he was later arrested. No stranger to violence, Kirby had already served time a few years before after attempting to murder his mother. This time, despite a recommendation for mercy, he was found guilty and executed on this day at Pentonville by Robert Baxter.

Grim Tales of Essex

King Louis XVIII of France spent two years (1807–8) of his exile at Gosfield Hall at the invitation of the Marquess of Buckingham. Living in exile in Westphalia when Louis XVI was guillotined in 1793, he declared himself Regent for his nephew, the boy King Louis XVII. When the 10-year-old king died in prison on 8 June 1795, Louis Stanislas Xavier proclaimed himself King Louis XVIII, and floated around Europe for the next few years until he finally gained the French throne in 1814. In accordance with French custom, some of Gosfield's locals would be allowed to watch the king dine – and it must have been quite a sight! Louis XVIII was undoubtedly the most hideously obese of all the Bourbons, and he made desperate attempts to deflect attention from his size by over-dressing in extravagant clothes. When the Prince Regent invested the new French king with the Order of the Garter, he discovered that Louis had an elephantine knee. The prince referred to the experience as like 'fastening a sash around a young man's waist'. Fleeing Paris for the hundred days after Napoleon's return, Louis took up his throne permanently after Napoleon's final defeat at Waterloo and remained king until his death on 16 September 1824.

13 OCTOBER **Essex Witches and Witchcraft**
Fire has long been supposed to be a potent 'draw' of witches. The villagers of Latchingdon suspected one of their number was a witch, who was performing malignant acts against local residents. They made a huge bonfire and stood around it silently. As it blazed to its height the old woman in question came along in great haste, whimpering and muttering as if in great pain, and made great efforts to make someone speak to her. All remained silent – for they knew if they spoke the 'draw' would break. Her discomfort grew with every crackle and spit of the fire until someone inadvertently spoke a few words. This broke the charm and the old woman, relieved from her pains, scuttled off home again.

14 OCTOBER **County Gaols and Bridewells of Essex visited by Prison Reformer John Howard**
In addition to the bridewell in Colchester Castle, which was reserved for prisoners from outlying areas, the town of Colchester also had a combined gaol and bridewell, which Howard visited in 1776, 1779 and 1782. There was a room for debtors, a strong ward for men and another for women, with two additional rooms added to the bridewell. The court was described as 'very offensive; no water in it', and there was no straw in the prison. An allowance of 3*d* a day fed and watered the prisoners, while a chaldron of coals was given for heating in the winter. The keeper was paid a salary of just £12.

15 OCTOBER **1839** On this day the inhabitants of Dunmow presented a petition to the Essex Quarter Sessions requesting efficient policing of the area. The justices accepted their petition, declaring that 'ordinary officers appointed for preserving the peace within the county were not sufficient for the peace and protection of the inhabitants and for the security of the property within the county'. Essex was one of the first eight counties of England to take advantage of the County Police Act, raising a force of 115 constables and superintendents. Captain John Bunch Bonnemaison McHardy was appointed Chief Constable in 1840 on a salary of £400.

16 OCTOBER **1779** The effigies of three carved wooden crusader knights dating from the fourteenth century recline in eternal slumber in Danbury Church. A curious tale relates to one of the nearby floor tombs, thought to be that of Sir Gerard de Braybrooke, who died on 14 March 1422. This tomb now bears only the indent of the 'cross fleury' brass which once adorned it. On this day in 1779 a grave was being dug in the north aisle for a member of the Ffytche family, when a lead coffin was discovered under the old slab. A group of interested gentlemen from Danbury were fetched and the lid of the coffin was removed, revealing a further resinous shell. When this lid was removed it revealed a man of about 5ft dressed in a linen shirt with a narrow 'rude' lace at the neck. The body appeared to be in a perfect state of preservation, to the degree that when touched the jaws of his mouth opened and revealed 'a set of perfectly white teeth'. It appeared the fine preservation was due to the substance in which the knight's body had been immersed, which was best described as a 'pickle of sorts' that resembled 'mushroom catsup'. Mr White, the local surgeon, whose sense of smell was poor, opted to taste the liquid and concluded it tasted of 'the pickle of Spanish olives'. The coffin was then resealed and re-interred, and Sir Gerard has rested in peace ever since.

One of the carved wooden knights of Danbury.

1872   One person was killed and sixteen injured when the 9.45 Yarmouth to London Express train left the rails just north of Kelvedon station and split in half, causing one of the carriages to topple over and roll down the embankment. Passengers complained that they felt the train suddenly 'drop' immediately before the accident; at the inquiry this was revealed to have been caused by the failure of the leading traverse springs of the engine – which in turn caused the accident.

17 OCTOBER

1016   *The Battle of Assandune.* This fierce clash between the armies of Canute the Dane and Edmund Ironside is said to have been fought in Essex, probably near the village now known as Ashingdon. Local folklore says that Canute was camped on Canewdon Hill, and Ironside drew up his men on Ashingdon Hill. Both armies then rushed down their hills at speed and clashed on the plain between. When the ground had been churned into a sea of mud and blood under the warriors' feet a halt was called to the battle, and Ironside issued a challenge of single combat with Canute

18 OCTOBER

The battlefield of Assandune.

The church
erected by Canute
at Ashingdon.

to settle the matter. Canute and his men were weary of fighting and so
Canute (who was allegedly much smaller than Ironside) suggested instead
that they divide the kingdom, with the Danes taking all that lay to the
north of Watling Street, the old Roman road which ran between Dover and
Chester, and Ironside taking everything to the south. This was agreed, but
Ironside's death less than two months later left Canute as overall King of
England. It has been suggested that Canute was behind Ironside's death.

1769 This day saw the death of Daniel Day (84), the eccentric originator of the annual Fairlop Fair. A block- and pump-maker from Wapping, Day owned a small estate not far from the great Fairlop Oak. On the first Friday in July he would travel there in a boat on wheels drawn by horses to collect his rents, and would end the day with a feast of beans and bacon. When his beloved Fairlop Oak lost a large branch, he had a coffin made out of it for his own interment, frequently entertaining his friends by 'trying it for size'. After Day's death the fair was still held, and by the 1830s it had become a grand occasion, with side-shows, performances and wheeled boats coming from as far away as London's East End: 'the roads leading to Ilford, and thence to the fair, presented a scene of animation and bustle from morn to night'.

The Fairlop Oak and Fair.

Essex Witches and Witchcraft

People on the margins of society, such as struggling widows or those with mental illness or deformity, have often been seen as good candidates for supposed witches. One eccentric old man in Mayland did nothing more than drive around in a light cart pulled by two huge dogs – and he was condemned as an undoubted witch who had turned two lost travellers into dogs for the purpose!

1949 On this day farm labourer Sidney Tiffen, wildfowling on Dengie Flats, found a large piece of a human body. It was examined by eminent pathologist Dr Francis Camps, who concluded that the body, with its head and legs missing, had been thrown onto the marshes from a plane. The 'Essex Torso' was eventually identified by its fingerprints as Stanley Setty, a small-time crook and gangland 'banker', who had been living at Lancaster Gate, London. Investigations revealed that on 5 October Brian Donald Hume had taken off in a hired Auster sports plane from the United Services' Flying Club at Elstree with two packages. Hume was another small-time crook who was known to the police. He was soon connected with Setty through various shady dealings, and evidence began to be amassed against Hume, who was eventually brought before the Old Bailey charged with the murder on 18 January 1950. Hume eventually plea-bargained and was found not guilty of murder, although he agreed to plead guilty to the lesser charge of being an accessory connected with the disposal of the body. He was sentenced to twelve years. As soon as he was released on remission in 1958 he sold his graphic story about how he murdered Setty to the *Sunday Pictorial*: 'I stood over him with a dripping, blood red dagger in my hand' ran part of his confession. He was soon back to his old tricks, working as an armed robber, and by January 1959 he was back on trial for killing a taxi-driver while fleeing from an abortive bank raid in Zurich. Switzerland has no death penalty so Hume escaped the noose again. In 1976 he was judged insane and returned to Britain, where he was confined in Broadmoor. He died there on 19 April 1988 aged 67.

22 OCTOBER   **1962**   Alfred Kemp (26) was brought before Essex Assizes charged with murdering his wife Shirley. In court he recounted the tragic story of how they had argued about his night shift work at Ford's plant in Dagenham. He had attempted to comfort her by placing his arm about her neck, but they both toppled to the floor and he felt her go limp. The jury returned a verdict of not guilty of murder and Kemp was discharged.

23 OCTOBER   **1881**   *The Saffron Walden Murder.* John Prior, one of Lord Braybrooke's principal gamekeepers, was shot in an exchange with a poacher on the Hunter's Well Plantation near Roos Farm. A good description of the man responsible was obtained from a witness and he was traced to a cottage on Elder Street, Wimbush. A number of men were found there, at least two of them from the Wright family, and they were all very alike to look at. The police officers sought out the various brothers in the village and confirmed the identity of their suspect as William Wright; he was found and arrested at his brother's house on the Thaxted road. Tried at Chelmsford Assizes, he was found guilty of firing the fatal shot and was sentenced to death (later commuted to penal servitude for life).

24 OCTOBER   **1840**   PC30 Josiah Hawkins Radley, the village constable of Sible Hedingham, was keeping an eye on the home of the Newmans, a local family of ne'er-do-wells, during the hours of darkness. Hearing footsteps, he hid himself in a hedgerow and watched as Mehuman Newman came into view, carrying a large sack over his shoulders. Immediately suspicious, Radley challenged Newman, demanding to know what was in the sack. Defiantly Newman kicked out at the policeman, who drew his truncheon and fended off his would-be assailant; Newman dropped the sack and ran home. Just as Radley realised the sack contained a dead sheep, Newman returned with his strongly built father, James (72), both carrying iron bars which they used against Radley before he had time to react. He was bludgeoned into unconsciousness and by the time he had come round again the sack and its contents were gone. Locals attended to the wounded constable and Superintendent Redin was sent for from Castle Hedingham. When he arrived he armed himself with a pistol before bursting into the Newmans' cottage and ordering them to come quietly. Brought before the magistrates, James got twelve months' hard labour for the assault and Mehuman received a month's hard labour for the assault and fifteen years' transportation for the theft of the sheep!

Old Punishments: Prisoners' Meals

25 OCTOBER

In 1916 the Essex police force stipulated the following regulations for prisoners' meals: 'They shall normally be served at 7.00am, 12.30pm and 6.30pm. Breakfast and tea shall consist of one pint of tea or coffee with milk and sugar and 8oz of bread. Dinner shall consist of 2oz of cheese in addition to the above. Drinking water to be supplied when requested. Relations or friends may supply them with meals but the food must be examined before it is given to them.'

Essex Witches and Witchcraft

26 OCTOBER

A report in the East London Advertiser in 1903 ran: 'A Bishop Stortford barber was cutting the hair of a customer from a neighbouring village when he was requested to save a piece of hair from the nape of the neck. The barber ascertained that the man imagined that someone in the village had done him an injury, and to have revenge he intended to cast a spell upon him; the hair from the nape of the neck, the lip, and the armpits, the parings of the nails and other ingredients mixed with water were to be corked up in a bottle and placed on a fire at night. Desiring sickness to fall upon his enemy, his wish would be accomplished as the bottle burst, which would be as near midnight as possible.'

Last Rites

27 OCTOBER

In the church of Little Parndon is a headstone to Hester Woodley, who died in 1767 in her 68th year. The stone is almost unique in Britain, for it marks the grave of an African woman who was sold into slavery. Hester faithfully served two generations of the Woodley family in the village; when Mrs Bridget, the lady of the house, died, her daughter had 'inherited' Hester.

Hester Woodley's gravestone.

1782 John Newman, the road toll collector at Hutton, was attacked by a highwayman in the twilight hours. Not satisfied by shooting Newman the instant he opened the door to his tollgate

28 OCTOBER

cottage, the 'gentleman of the road' went on to beat Newman senseless. He then made off with not only the toll money but also Newman's few personal valuables. Newman died of his wounds a few days after the horrific attack. Despite widely circulated posters offering £100 reward for information leading to the apprehension of the villain responsible, the culprit was never identified.

29 OCTOBER **Grim Tales of Essex**
In 1789 Richard Savill robbed and killed fellow-villager Thomas Bray. Tried and hanged for his crime, Savill was gibbeted on Manuden Common – facing his mother's cottage!

30 OCTOBER **The Witchfinder-General: Divining a Witch's Imp or Familiar**
The Revd John Gaule recorded the methods of Matthew Hopkins and his searchers in 1646: 'Having taken the suspected witch, she is placed in

a room upon a stool or table cross-legged, or in some other uneasy posture, to which if she submits not she is then bound with cords; there she is watched and kept without meat or sleep for the space of 24 hours for within that time they shall see her imp come and suck. . . . A little hole is likewise made in the door for the imp to come in at; and lest at night come in some discernable shape, they that watch are taught to be ever and anon sweeping the room and if they see spiders or flies, to kill them. And if they cannot kill them, then they may be sure they are imps.'

A witch and her 'familiars'.

31 OCTOBER **1849** Saffron Walden's High Constable, William Campling, was just opening the door to his home on Bridge Street when he was blasted with a shotgun, causing fatal wounds to his legs. Staggering inside, he said to his horrified family, 'Go and see where Pettit was, or where he had been.' Benjamin Pettit was known to bear a grudge against Campling, who had arrested him on a previous occasion. Within the hour Pettit was in custody. On 9 November Campling died of his wounds and Pettit was charged with murder. No witnesses came forward and no corroborative evidence could be produced against Pettit, so when he stood trial he was found not guilty and

freed.

NOVEMBER

PCs Collins and Lancum disguised for 'special duty' as
stevedores on Tilbury Docks with the intention of infiltrating
an illicit trade in intoxicating liquor, 1901.
(Essex Police Museum)

1 NOVEMBER **1961** Rose Vera Baker (34) was brought before Essex Assizes charged with strangling Martha McGee, a fellow inmate in the mental hospital where Rose had been a patient for the past seven years. Her 'explanation' for the killing was that she had been annoyed by McGee's singing. Baker was found unfit to plead and was detained at Her Majesty's pleasure.

2 NOVEMBER **1926** Hashankhan Scamander (36) was executed on this day for the murder of Khannar Jung Baz. On Friday 9 July 1926 Baz had been on watch aboard the SS *China* in Tilbury Docks with his cabin-mate Aslam Zardad, and both had then retired to their cabin to rest. Baz went to sleep first, and just as Zardad was drifting off he saw Scamander creep inside the cabin, and before he realised what was happening he saw the flash of a blade as Scamander stabbed Baz. When Scamander crept out again Zardad quietly followed him and made his way to the second engineer's cabin to raise the alarm. There had been bad blood between the two sailors for some time: two months before the stabbing Baz had been fined for attacking Scamander with hair-clippers, and the situation had not improved since that time. Scamander was found guilty of murder and executed by Robert Baxter at Pentonville.

3 NOVEMBER **1865** The newspapers on this day carried reports of Gunner Roach of the 1st Division, Depot Brigade, Royal Artillery, stationed at Sheerness, who was formally drummed out of the regiment. He had been found guilty of stealing various articles from the sergeants' mess and other dishonourable conduct; he had appeared before courts martial on two previous occasions. His offences were read out before a full parade on the drill square, then his buttons and stripes were cut off and the band played him off in disgrace. Roach was then taken to Springfield Gaol for 168 days' imprisonment.

4 NOVEMBER **1914** Charles Frembd (71) and his wife Louisa (52) ran a small grocer's shop on Harrow Road, Leytonstone. Their marriage was not a happy one and they frequently argued. On the morning of 28 August their domestic servant became concerned when the Frembds failed to appear at the usual time. She went to their bedroom, where she discovered Louisa lying on the bed, covered in blood. Charles was lying next to her, bleeding from a stab wound. Charles eventually recovered from his wound and stood trial for the murder of his wife. He stated that when she had started nagging at him in the night he 'snapped' and stabbed her and then attempted to take his own life the same way. Although medical opinions agreed that Frembd was suffering from senile decay, he was deemed culpable for his actions and was sent to the gallows. He was executed at Chelmsford prison on this day by executioner John Ellis. Frembd holds the dubious distinction of being the last man to be hanged in Essex as well as the oldest man to be hanged in Britain during the twentieth century.

5 NOVEMBER **1888** The villagers of Stebbing paraded and then ceremonially burnt a guy in the form of their unpopular village constable, PC Enoch Raison. Raison had been on the Essex force since 1851. He was well past retirement but was granted an extension of his service at his own request and was sent as the village constable to Stebbing. He made no attempt to ingratiate himself with the populace and they found him 'morose, officious, sharp-tongued and off-hand'. In October 1888 his superintendent at Dunmow received a notice warning him that if he did not remove Raison the villagers would do it for him! Their threats culminated in the parade and burning of the Raison-guy on their bonfire. On 23 November 1888 PC Raison was persuaded to accept his pension and move away from Stebbing.

1879 Reported on this day was the case of John Douglas Spence (13) and Henry Silver (14), who were charged with twice attempting to set fire to the training ship *Shaftesbury* in early August. No evidence was offered against Silver, who was ordered to be discharged. No reason could be assigned to Spence's act, and his captain even wrote a letter describing his previous good character. However, he was sentenced to ten days' imprisonment and twelve strokes of the birch rod, and afterwards was to be sent to a reformatory for three years.

6 NOVEMBER

Grim Tales of Essex

It is hard to imagine today, but when the Salvation Army embarked on its first parades and marches in Essex in 1882 they were very unpopular. Mud and stones were hurled at the Salvationists by locals who did not

7 NOVEMBER

A Salvation Army Band.

appreciate their moralising, especially about drinking. Such was the aggression shown in Harwich that a man was arrested and charged with assaulting a Salvation Army corporal. In Colchester the corporation tried to introduce a bylaw to prevent the Salvation Army's parades, and complaints were lodged about the police manpower needed to guard the processions. Borough officers were eventually told to escort the processions only if they passed through their beats – if the Salvation Army wanted more protection they would have to pay for it!

8 NOVEMBER

Witch 'pricking' devices.

The Witchfinder-General: Finding the Devil's Mark

It was believed that every witch bore a 'Devil's Mark', an area on the skin insensible to pain which showed 'beyond doubt' the bearer had entered into a diabolical contract with the Devil. Sometimes in the shape of a toad's foot, a hare, a puppy or a spider, it would be imprinted on the most secret parts of the body. In men it could be under the eyelids, on the lips, in the armpits or the anus, while in women 'it is generally on the breasts and private parts'. If a mark 'proved invisible', the suspected witch would be shaved all over to ensure no mark was hidden by her hair. Blindfolded, the alleged witch would then be 'pricked' all over by a type of crooked bodkin (about 4in long), which would be thrust all over the usual suspect areas of the body where a mark could be hid. If an area was found insensible to the pain of pricking, it was seen as incontrovertible proof that the person was a witch.

9 NOVEMBER

1821 William Thorp, a fair-stall holder, was returning from Epping on the way to Harlow Bush Fair on this moonless night when he was surrounded by about ten men. One clasped his hands over his mouth from behind, while others held his arms and legs and rifled through his pockets. A young man Thorp identified by his voice as Joseph Binder (17) caught hold of Thorp's fob, proclaiming 'You have got a roll of notes here' and tore them away; they were in fact memorandums. Having taken all they could, one of the gang kicked Thorp on the breech and told him he could now go about his business. Upwards of twenty persons were robbed and 'ill-used' at the fair that night. Joseph Binder was tried at the Lent Assizes for his involvement in the assault and highway robbery; found guilty, he was sentenced to death.

10 NOVEMBER

1750 Edward Bright of Maldon died on this day. Born in the town on 1 March 1721, he worked as a post-boy riding to Chelmsford and back every day, and soon developed a keen appetite. By the time he was 11 he weighed 10 stone. When he was 12 he was apprenticed to learn the art of the grocer – not the wisest career choice for a young man who liked his food. However, he did well and within ten years he was running his own grocer's and tallow chandler's shop. He was still eating massive meals and had acquired a taste for mature, strong ales and drank about a pint of wine a day. At 22 he weighed 30 stone, and by 28 he tipped the scales at 41 stone. Now morbidly obese, Bright began to suffer with shortness of breath, inflammation of the legs and fevers. Each time he fell ill his doctor would

The wager where
seven 'hundred'
men were buttoned
into Edward Bright's
waistcoat (each of the
seven men came from
Dengie Hundred).

bleed him of two pints of blood, after which he was usually 'much restored'.
He contracted typhus in late October 1750 and died in his bed. At the time
of his demise Bright measured 6ft 11in around the belly, 2ft 8in round the
middle of his legs and 2ft 2in round the middle of his arms, but stood just
5ft 9in tall. There was no way his gargantuan coffin would go down the
stairs in his house, and a hole had to be cut through the wall and staircase
to remove it. He was interred in a vault near the tower of All Saints'
Church with the aid of a specially built heavy-duty triangle and pulleys.

11 NOVEMBER

The surrendered
U-boat fleet at
Harwich, 1918.

1918 *Armistice Day.* At the eleventh hour of the eleventh day of the eleventh month the guns at last fell silent as the First World War came to an end. The German High Seas Fleet surrendered at Scapa Flow, while the U-boat submarine flotillas (consisting of more than 150 submarines and 2 smaller vessels) were handed over to the Harwich Naval Force led by Commodore Reginald Tyrwhitt.

12 NOVEMBER

1897 *The 'Black Monday' Storm and Flood.* A massive gale whipped up high tides and caused extensive damage to shipping, property and farmland all along the east coast. In Essex it was estimated that 50,000 acres of land were flooded, with Canvey Island, Great Wakering, Bowers Gifford and Burnham-on-Crouch suffering most. Railway lines were swept away, the bathing machines at Southend 'floated about like cockleshells', and ten soldiers in two boats at Shoeburyness barracks were swept out to sea and ended up in Kent – they were lucky to survive.

13 NOVEMBER

1945 The trial of James McNichol (30), a sergeant at the Heavy Anti-Aircraft Battery at Thorpe Bay, opened at Chelmsford on this day. At a dance in the evening of 16 August 1945 he was annoyed to see his girlfriend dancing with some RAF men, and fellow-sergeants Donald Kirkaldie and Leonard Cox. McNichol seemed unable to calm down about it. Later on, when Kirkaldie and Cox were back in the Nissen hut they shared with two other men, one of the hut's windows was suddenly shattered in the small hours of the 17th. A hand was seen curling in through the broken pane, then the light was switched on and seconds later the muzzle of a rifle appeared through the same aperture and shots rang out. Cox was wounded but Kirkaldie, hit in the throat, died instantly. McNichol was soon identified as the guilty party and was arrested the same day. He claimed he had simply fired into the hut to frighten Cox and Kirkaldie, but the jury were not convinced and found him guilty of murder. McNichol was executed by Albert Pierrepoint at Pentonville on Friday 21 December 1945.

1895 William Cable (35), a member of the sect known as the 'Peculiar People', was charged at the Assizes with neglecting his four children in such a manner as to cause unnecessary suffering or be injurious to their health. It was stated that during the diphtheria epidemic at Rayleigh in the previous spring Cable's children were all stricken with the illness. He did not call in any medical man to attend to them because to do so would have been contrary to his religious beliefs. Instead they were nursed and prayed over by members of the sect. All four children died. The jury did not feel the prisoner had wilfully neglected his children but had acted within his beliefs, and they acquitted Mr Cable.

14 NOVEMBER

Essex Witches and Witchcraft

A poor elderly couple in the early nineteenth century named Hart were known to their local community in Fambridge as a witch and a wizard. A few folk sought them out for leechcraft and cures, but they were eventually set upon by a group of locals who were convinced the couple contrived mischievous acts and brought misfortunes upon the people of the district. The Harts were dragged to the local pond and 'swum' to ascertain if they really were witches. The old man was pronounced innocent when he nearly drowned in the test, but the woman was tied to a boat by a line and floated – thus 'proved' a witch, she was persecuted and mistrusted for the few short years she had left before she died.

15 NOVEMBER

County Gaols and Bridewells of Essex visited by Prison Reformer John Howard

Harwich Town Gaol was visited in 1778. It consisted of two rooms facing the street and had no chimneys. There was a back room called the 'dark gaol' and another with a fireplace. It had no court for exercise, no water supply and no sewer. Prisoners were each allowed 3½d for food every day. The keeper's salary was £2 8s and fees per prisoner stood at 6s 8d.

16 NOVEMBER

1817 George Waller (15), a labouring boy who was unable to read or write, was charged with setting fire to four stacks of wheat, three stacks of barley and a quantity of other produce, the property of his master George Cockerill, and to several farm buildings, the property of Viscount Maynard at Great Easton. He was found guilty of setting the fires, and the judge felt 'he was bound to inflict such a punishment as would be calculated to deter others'.

17 NOVEMBER

He thus sentenced Waller to ten years' penal servitude where, he said, the boy 'might receive instruction, and become a useful member of society'.

18 NOVEMBER **1872** Thomas Dudley, gamekeeper to Sir Thomas Western, Lord Lieutenant of Essex, was fatally shot by poachers while he patrolled the estate at Great Braxted. Dudley's fellow-gamekeepers had a good idea who was responsible and summoned the police. Three men were arrested, including William Bundock, who was thought to have fired the fatal shot. Evidence was found all over his house, in the shape of wet clothes, powder and shot in his jacket pockets and a shotgun under his bed. All three men were removed to Witham police station. At the inquest a verdict of wilful murder was pronounced and Bundock was sent for trial. However, the jury decided that the gun had been discharged in panic at being discovered and not with intent to murder. Bundock was an old offender, and the judge told him he was lucky to be acquitted of the capital charge; however, found guilty of poaching with violence, he was sentenced to five years' penal servitude. Bundock's non-violent accomplices, Challis and Miller, both received four months with hard labour.

19 NOVEMBER **1833** A woman was brought before the magistrates in Essex charged with witchcraft. One prosecution witness gave evidence on oath that the accused woman could fly. The judge in reply said, 'So she might, if she would', as he knew no law against it. The case was dismissed.

20 NOVEMBER **Grim Tales of Essex**
In November 1778 the notorious Essex smuggler William Dowsett sailed to the French coast and took 2 ankers and 391 half-ankers (a total of about 1,600 gallons) of brandy, rum and gin on board his cutter *Neptune*, and then set sail back to England. Winding up the Whitaker Channel off the Crouch estuary, *Neptune* was spotted by the Revenue cutter *Bee*. As they intercepted the smuggler's vessel, the revenue men demanded to search the vessel, a demand that was vehemently refused again and again. Captain Hart of the Bee had no option but to fire a warning shot across the *Neptune*'s bows. After an exchange of fire two of the leading smugglers were killed and the rest of the crew were forced to yield to the duty men.

21 NOVEMBER **1887** Joseph Morley (17) was hanged at Springfield Gaol by executioner James Berry for the murder of Mrs Rogers, a young married woman with whom he lodged at Chigwell Row, Dagenham. After sentence was passed, Morley admitted his crime – he cut her throat with a razor he found in her bedroom – but denied that he had had any intention to kill her before he entered the room.

22 NOVEMBER **1953** As a result of enquiries by his mother-in-law and subsequent interrogation by Detective Sergeant Sewell of South Benfleet, Albert Edward Kemp (30) admitted that his wife Audrey Olive Kemp (24) had died during a struggle while she was in a fit of temper. It had happened the previous July while Kemp was serving as a sergeant in the Royal Artillery at Weybourne Military Camp, Norfolk. Not knowing what to do, he had placed the body in a tin trunk – where it had remained ever since. When he moved to Benfleet after demobilisation, he put the trunk inside a wooden packing case and brought it with him. The body was found in the trunk with a silk stocking tied round its neck. Kemp was charged with murder but he was acquitted after he insisted the death was an accident, and claimed that he had tied the silk stocking round the neck so that it would look like murder because at the time he wished to die too.

23 NOVEMBER

1908 The *Marlborough*, a Thames Conservancy ship, tore away from her moorings in a gale and drifted on the turbulent waters; eventually it smashed clean through Southend Pier, leaving a gaping hole and substantial structural damage in its wake; it caused over £650-worth of damage. This was not the first time the pier had been damaged by shipping: there had been incidents in 1895, 1898 and 1907. There have been subsequent collisions too, in 1921 and 1986, as well as fires in 1976 and 1995. Some people are beginning to wonder if Southend Pier is jinxed!

The gap smashed through Southend Pier, 1908.

24 NOVEMBER

Essex Witches and Witchcraft

The sixteenth-century Court Book of Romford notes the confession of James Hopkins of Hornchurch, 'that he went to Mother Persore, at Navestoke, a connynge woman, to know by what means his master's cattle were bewitched'. He was ordered to appear before the next sessions. Another man, John Shonke of Romford, was revealed to have gone 'to Father Parfoothe for help with his wife, which Parfoothe is suspected to be a wiche. The said Shonke allowed it, and said he should do the like again, while Parfoothe is counted to be a wiche, and is allowed for a good wiche.' The judge received the confession and enjoined him to do public penance in the chapel in time of divine service, 'confessing him heartily sorry for seeking help of man and refusing the help of God'.

25 NOVEMBER   **1856**   Samuel Summers (20) appeared at the Central Criminal Court charged with having effected an escape from custody. Sentenced to a year in prison for stealing lead, he was transported under escort by railway to Chelmsford to serve his sentence at Springfield Gaol. The prisoner's wrists were cuffed but he was not cuffed to the officer, and as he clambered out of the train he darted away from his escort. Dashing down the stairs leading from the platform, he made his escape. Remaining at large for some months, he was said to have 'conducted himself respectably' and had even been employed until the police were tipped off about his whereabouts. Summers was told he still had to serve his year in prison and was given an extra month for his escape.

Winstanley's Lighthouse 1696

26 NOVEMBER   **1703**   The 'Great Channel Storm' claimed the lives of about eight thousand people across England and numerous ships were sunk or severely damaged as they smashed against harbour walls. The most famous Essex man to die in this terrible storm was the Saffron Walden-born inventor Henry Winstanley, who was lost when his lighthouse on the Eddystone rock 14 miles off Plymouth was destroyed by the storm.

27 NOVEMBER   **Essex Witches and Witchcraft**
In the late nineteenth century an Essex man was talking to a neighbour whose wife was a witch, when he happened

to make an out-of-turn comment. Within hours of his return home he was attacked by a host of fleas that stayed with him for days – but did not spread to any other member of his family. Consulting a cunning woman in the next village, he was advised to hang his coat in the corner of the chimney overnight, and whatever was inside it in the morning should be thrown on the fire. Come the morning a large toad was found in the coat; it was promptly thrown on the fire, where it exploded like gunpowder and on that instant the fleas dropped dead off the man like fine black sand.

1838 Susanna Playle, the widow of a Mountnessing innkeeper, decided after her husband's death to run the business herself. She was assisted in this by a family friend, Abraham Hilliard, who, as the months went by, began to demonstrate his affections for her. Susanna rebuffed the advances with good humour but Hilliard pressed further and would not take no for an answer. His romantic advances eventually became drink-fuelled threats and they argued. Susanna threw him out, shouting 'Never let me see your face again', to which he replied, 'Damn you, if you do not have me you will not have any other man.' A short while later Susanna's son John saw Hilliard entering the outside bakehouse where Susanna was working. John followed and was just in time to see Hilliard shoot Susanna. As John wrestled Hilliard to the ground, poor Susanna breathed her last. Hilliard was tried, found guilty and executed the following March. In front of a crowd of nearly three thousand people, he faintly spoke his last words: 'Goodbye, goodbye all; I hope I shall meet you in heaven.'

28 NOVEMBER

1851 The fire which gutted Mr Viall's hairdresser's shop in Manningtree was the talk of the town. Viall himself had narrowly escaped with his life from an upstairs window. The fire had been started deliberately, after a

29 NOVEMBER

cord tied to a gimlet had been used to secure the door. Closer examination revealed that the holes through which the cord was fastened had been made from the inside, and it was then revealed that Mr Viall had only recently insured his shop and its contents for inflated amounts of money.

30 NOVEMBER   1850   PC Robert Bamborough died of his injuries. He was escorting William Wood, a prisoner, along Church Lane, Hutton, when Wood turned on him and fought to escape. Both men tumbled into the pond, and Wood repeatedly forced handfuls of mud into the policeman's mouth until he lost consciousness and let go. But Wood wasn't a vindictive man, and he ran back and lifted the struggling policeman's head out of the water before making off. Bamborough was subsequently carried to the Chequers public house, where he died on this day. Wood was captured at Chatham and stood trial for murder. Luckily for him, two young witnesses had seen him return to the stricken copper and lift his head out of the water, and so he was saved from the gallows. Found guilty of manslaughter, Wood was transported for life.

Three Essex constables, 1914.

DECEMBER

St John's Abbey Gate, Colchester. After Henry VIII's split
with Rome he ordered the dissolution of the monasteries and
claimed for himself the properties, wealth, rights and tithes
of all the religious houses in Britain. When St John's Abbey
in Colchester was asked to surrender to his edict, Abbot
John Beche refused. He was invited to a feast, where he was
arrested. He was subsequently hanged near his own abbey
on 1 December 1539.

1 December **1903** In 1901 Bernard White was serving as a soldier in the 2nd Battalion, Essex Regiment. He had been 'walking out' with Maud Garrett for six weeks before he was sent overseas to serve in the Boer War, but on his return he found Maude was engaged to a soldier in the Medical Corps. White remained in the army, and a chance meeting in 1903 saw the pair arrange a moonlight assignation near his camp at Little Warley, Brentford. White sneaked out of camp at about 10.15pm and returned to his tent at 11.00pm. A gamekeeper later stated he heard screams at 10.45pm. The body of Maud Garrett was discovered at Warley Gap at about 5.00am by a passing labourer on his way to work; she had been battered to death. White was soon traced and blood was found on his boots, socks, trousers and cane. Tried and found guilty, 21-year-old White was executed on this day at Springfield Gaol, Chelmsford, by William Billington, assisted by Henry Pierrepoint.

2 December **1859** George Currey (29), a post office letter carrier at Braintree, pleaded guilty at the Winter Assizes to stealing a letter containing three half-sovereigns. The judge, keen that an example be made of Currey, sentenced him to four years' penal servitude.

3 December **1856** The Revd William Palm, Rector of Stifford, and his family came downstairs to discover the ground floor of their house had been burgled and ransacked. More distressingly, it appeared the robbers had piled up some papers with the intention of setting fire to them; luckily the flames had gone out with 'little mischief caused'. If it had caught hold, the potential consequences for the rector and his family would have been unthinkable. George Polley was arrested soon afterwards when some of the stolen property was found on him, and his fate was sealed when his knife was found at the scene of the crime. Polley was brought before the Spring Assizes and charged with 'burglariously' breaking and entering the dwelling house and stealing a knife and other items from the property; found guilty, he was sentenced to fifteen years' transportation.

4 December **1894** This day saw the execution of James Canham Read, the 'Southend Murderer', at Springfield Gaol, Chelmsford. A middle-aged book-keeper with a wife and eight children, Read also had a string of mistresses. One of these was pretty Florence Dennis, aged just 18. When she fell pregnant, she had no hesitation in naming Read as the father and wrote to him asking what he proposed to do about it. He arranged to meet her in Southend. When she did not return from the meeting, her concerned sister (who had also been one of Read's mistresses!) wrote to him to enquire if he could shed light on Florence's whereabouts. In a panic, Read stole some money from his office and fled (with another mistress) to Mitcham in Surrey. Meanwhile, Florence's body was recovered from a field at Prittlewell. She had been shot. Read was traced and arrested. He was found guilty of her murder at Chelmsford Assizes and duly paid the ultimate price. Later, J. Holt Schooling, a member of Lord Egerton's Committee on the Mental and Physical Condition of Children, was to comment that Read had the face of a murderer: 'not even the most casual observer can fail to see it . . . [his face causes] a feeling of aversion and distrust'.

WILFUL MURDER

WANTED

For the Murder of Florence Dennis at
Southend-on-Sea, 24th June. 1894

JAMES CANHAM READ

Cashier, Royal Albert Docks. London.

Age 39,   Height 5ft 7in,
Hair Brown,
Moustache Slight Brown,
Small Side Whiskers,
Eyes Brown and prominent,
Complexion Fresh,
Two Upper Front Teeth
project slightly,
One overlaps the other.

DRESS,
Dark Brown Hard Felt Hat,
Short Black Coat and Vest,
Light Grey Trousers,
Walks Quickly,
Is of very smart and
Gentlemanly appearance.

Has a Gold Watch engraved inside case " Presented
to Mr. James Canham Read by his fellow Clerks, Royal
Albert Docks, London."

WARRANT ISSUED.

Information to be sent to
SUPT. HAWTREE, Southend-on-Sea.

FRANCIS & SONS, Printers, &c., 55, High Street. Southend and Rochford.

Wanted poster for James Canham Read. *(Essex Police Museum)*

5 December **1899** Execution of Samuel Crozier (35) at Springfield Gaol, Chelmsford. The landlord of the Admiral Ross Inn at Galleywood Common, Chelmsford, Crozier had not been long married when he was seen to knock his wife off the sofa, kick her and beat her during an argument in a room above the pub. She died the next morning. The doctor who attended was told she had acquired her injuries as a result of a fall, and recorded death by 'natural causes'. However, the violence of the previous night was reported to the police and Crozier was initially charged with manslaughter and later murder. Found guilty of murder, he was sent to the gallows and was executed by James and William Billington. He showed no real contrition, and when asked if he had anything to say before sentence was carried out he replied, 'No sir, nothing than I have already said at the trial.'

6 December **1830** *An orderly riot.* A group of about forty farm labourers marched on the farm of Mr Ford in the parish of St Michael, near Colchester; after issuing warnings that 'he should know when it was dark' to the farmer's son here, they proceeded to John Turner's farm at Mile End. William Hardwick stated their demands to Turner for increased wages of 2s a day and beer to be provided up to Lady Day, and concluded: 'It is all we wish to have. We will have it by fair means or foul.' Turner said he understood the need for more money to support large families but pointed out that his overheads were so heavy he could give them no more. Concerned by the threatened disturbance, and fearing for his wife who had only recently given birth, he signed the demand sheet Hardwick presented to him. The mob then went on to the farms of Mr Winckall and Mr Nunn, gathering more and more labourers to their cause along the way. As they left Nunn's farm, the protesting labourers numbered about a hundred. They were met by a mounted party of magistrates and special constables under the direction of Sir Henry Smith. The men respectfully repeated their demands and Sir Henry promised he would see the matter considered. The assembled labourers did not want an outright confrontation with lawmen and duly dispersed. Those considered the ringleaders in the 'riot' were arrested and tried at the Winter Assizes. All received good character references but such insurrection was not to be tolerated, and all were found guilty of riot. William Hardwick and another man named James Wright both received twelve months' imprisonment; eight others received custodial sentences of between three and nine months, all with hard labour.

7 December **1895** PC Hagger was brought before Saffron Walden Petty Sessions and found guilty of 'exceeding his duty'. He was fined 10s and ordered to pay 11s costs.

8 December **1943** *The Layer Marney Taxi Cab Murder.* Two US servicemen, J.C. Leatherberry and George Fowler, came up with what they thought was a foolproof get-rich-quick scheme. They would catch a taxi and ask the driver to take them to a secluded spot; there they would rob him and then run off into the

Police mugshots of
J.C. Leatherberry.
(Essex Police Museum)

darkness. On the night of 7 December, after 11.00pm, they duly picked up a taxi driven by Colchester resident Harry Hailstone (28), but before they got to a suitable spot Fowler asked the driver to pull over because he was desperate to urinate. When he returned to the roadside he saw Leatherberry and the taxi driver locked in a desperate struggle, in which Leatherberry savagely beat and strangled poor Harry Hailstone to death. The pair then set about concealing the body; they pushed it under a wire fence and watched it roll down a slope, and then they drove off in the taxi, dumping it at Hayes Green Lane, Layer Marney. After some keen detective work Fowler and Leatherberry were traced, and bloodstained clothes were recovered from Leatherberry's locker. Both men stood trial at a court martial in Ipswich Town Hall and both were found guilty. Fowler received a life sentence while Leatherberry was executed on 16 March 1944 at Shepton Mallet Prison, Somerset.

1893   An inquest was held into the circumstances of the fire which gutted Welch's tailor's and outfitter's in Short Wyre Street, Colchester. The charred remains of its owner, Alfred Welch, had been discovered lying face down on the workroom stairs. At the inquest Welch's foreman, Henry Sizzey, stated that Mr Welch had told him a former employee named Arthur Blatch had wanted a private meeting saying, 'something terrible is going to happen'. Sizzey assumed that because Blatch's wife had recently left him, he was going to ask Mr Welch for money to go after her. Evidence was also given

9 December

Arthur Blatch.

to the effect that the cash box recovered from the fire was £100 short. The inquest was adjourned pending further enquiries. The post-mortem performed by Dr Becker and Police Surgeon Maybury revealed foul play: Welch's skull had been fractured. A bloodstained crowbar was also recovered from the scene. Blatch was a prime suspect, and a man answering his description had been seen acting suspiciously in the area; the same man was also seen catching an early train at Witham. A verdict of wilful murder was returned in absentia against Arthur Blatch, but where was he? The Watch Committee offered a reward of £50 for his arrest and hundreds of handbills carrying his description were circulated across the country. He was never traced.

10 DECEMBER 1827 This day saw the first execution at the new Springfield Gaol. Reuben Martin (aka James Winter) went to a sale of clothes of a man who had suddenly died (the proceeds of the sale would be used to compensate the parish after it had had to meet the man's funeral costs) at the Yorkshire Grey pub in Colchester. Isaac Parsons also attended the sale, and purchased a coat. As he and his wife were leaving the sale, they were accosted by Martin and a group of other men, all the worse for drink, and an altercation broke out. Thomas Patrick, the landlord, summoned the constable, and by the time he arrived a fight was in progress at the corner of Water Lane. Martin, known in the area as 'Big Jem', was a hefty man and would not come quietly, becoming more violent as the officer attempted to arrest him. Freeing himself from the constable's grasp, Martin grabbed a large piece of rail fence and struck Mr Patrick a terrific blow on the head. The publican immediately dropped to the ground and did not rise again. Martin went berserk and ran up the street chasing witnesses and threatening to 'knock your bloody brains out!' He was eventually caught a few hours later in Coggeshall Grove. Tired and bloody, this time he came quietly. Indifferent to the charge or his fate, Martin was found guilty of the murder of Thomas Patrick and was sentenced to death. After the execution, his body was left to hang for an hour and was then handed over to the prison surgeon for dissection, a process that was viewed by a number of prominent local men.

11 DECEMBER 1828 *Death of Sir Gilbert East.* Sir Gilbert left very specific and quite peculiar directions for his funeral and burial. His next of kin were to see that he was

buried at Witham in the family vault beneath St Nicholas's Church, and were to order for him a cedarwood coffin adorned with Russian leather and half-filled with camphor and spices. The body was to be placed in this prepared coffin and then the whole sealed up and put in a wrought-iron coffin painted with six layers of black paint 'embellished with armorial and funereal devices richly'. Then Sir Gilbert was to be laid next to the coffin of his wife and the two encircled with a brass band inscribed: 'Whom God has joined together let no man put asunder.' The elaborate funeral ceremonies and feasting were to spread over almost a week. However, there was a problem. Sir Gilbert had specifically requested that he be 'buried in woollen', but this crucial request had been omitted so the poor man had to be disinterred, dressed according to his wishes and laid to rest again. Let's hope he has rested in peace ever since.

1880 At 1.00am Charles Murrells (56), Caleb Farran (40) and William Gaskin (45) broke into the home of Thomas Cole, a butcher, residing at Hare Green, Great Bromley. Mr Cole heard the sound of breaking glass, and went to the door just in time to see one of the men put his hand through the smashed pane and begin to turn the key in the lock. As they made their way to the sitting room, Cole saw that each of the burglars was disguised with a black net over his face. As he attempted to make his escape, Cole was tripped up by a fourth man and struck on the head with a thick stick by a fifth, whom he later identified as Farran. Cole was taken back inside and his money located and taken with intimidation. Murrells was caught first. On the day after the burglary he was in a pub where he made it known he had a sovereign and a 'bit of paper' – a £5 note! As a cattle market drover

12 December

he could hardly have come by such money legitimately. It was soon found he had made enquiries about Cole's business in the days before the attack. Apprehended a few days later, he made a desperate attack on the arresting officer with a knife. Two of the other burglars were soon in custody and the three were brought to trial at the January Assizes. The case against Gaskin was very circumstantial and he was acquitted. Farran was given fifteen years and Murrell, who had a number of previous convictions (including a sentence of fifteen years for aggravated burglary), was sent down for life.

13 December **1823** John Pallett was executed on this day before a large crowd in the walled space between Moulsham Gaol and the river at Chelmsford. Pallett had been employed by Mr Mumford of Widdington since boyhood, but sadly he bore a grudge against Mr Mumford's son John ('Jem'), who had punished Pallett for lopping his father's trees and committing other trespasses. Pallett needed only a few drinks to declare he 'would do for young Mumford'. According to his condemned cell confession, Pallett had been drinking at the Coach and Horses, Quendon, and much the worse for drink he had set out with another man named Kidman to fetch sand from Newport. As they passed Quendon Want-Lane Kidman spotted Jem Mumford and pointed him out to Pallett, who said angrily, 'Damn him, he shall have it!' Fuelled with drink, Pallett went after Mumford, and struck him about the head with a stick he had cut from a hedge. When young Mumford was on the floor helpless, Pallett cut his throat with a knife. Then he made off with Mumford's coat and a few personal items. Arriving at a nearby turnip field, Pallett sat down and reflected on his crime. Wracked with pangs of guilt, he went back to the body, put it over his shoulder and began to carry it back to Widdington; he was apparently under the impression that he could convince the Mumford family he had actually found the boy's body and carried him back home as a good deed. He met a few other men on the road and together they got the body back to Mrs Whisken's pub, where it was put in a chair and identified as Jem Mumford. When Pallett left the tap-room to clean himself up, the others quickly realised what had happened and Pallett was taken into custody. Found guilty of the crime, Pallett walked firmly onto the scaffold, where the executioner shook him strongly by his clasped hands and was kind enough to swing on his legs after the trap dropped to speed him on his way. 'The crowd were perfectly silent, and looked on with awe, but not sympathy.'

14 December **1864** John Williams, a labourer, was brought before the Winter Assizes charged with setting fire to a stack of wheat and two stacks of straw at St Osyth. Found guilty of the crime and reprimanded by the judge for his actions, he was sentenced to fifteen years' penal servitude. The unrepentant Williams, on hearing his sentence, said, 'Thank you my Lord, it's the best day's work I ever did in my life.'

15 December **1912** The 'Brightlingsea Tragedy' and the subsequent inquest and funerals were the talk of the town. The American Junius Booth, a descendant of

John Wilkes Booth (the man who assassinated President Lincoln), was the manager of the cinematograph theatre in the town. He and his wife Florence were a quiet and respectable couple who rented furnished apartments from Mrs Stebbings at 19 Tower Street. On Friday 6 December Mrs Stebbings heard a strange noise in the couple's room, and on hearing their dog whining went to investigate. She was shocked to discover Mr and Mrs Booth shot in their bed. Police Sergeant Brett stated at the inquest that when he arrived on the scene a revolver was lying on Mrs Booth's breast near Mr Booth's right hand. Mrs Booth had been shot behind the left ear, while Mr Booth had clearly placed the revolver in his mouth and fired it. A letter found in the bedroom was read out at the inquest: 'I have given my wife a sleeping draft to ease her pain. Cannot make her answer. Have given her an overdose. I am nearly mad. Cannot live without her; so I shall take the same.' After giving the name of his executor and the whereabouts of relevant papers, the letter was signed J.B. A verdict of murder and suicide was recorded.

Essex Witches and Witchcraft

16 December

James Murrell, known to most people as 'Cunning Murrell', stood no more than 5ft tall but was arguably one of the most powerful witches Essex had ever seen. Born in Rayleigh but settled in Hadleigh, it was said he could 'do anything, cure anything and know anything, past, present and future'.

Witches flying to their sabbat.

In hushed voices locals said that he possessed the evil eye, and that once in a magical duel he summoned up all his powers and ordered his opponent to die – and die he did! Murrell said: 'There will be witches at Leigh-on Sea for 100 years, three in Hadleigh and nine in Canewdon for ever'; he was witchmaster of them all and could summon the witches to their sabbat in Canewdon churchyard by whistling. Villagers wishing to consult Murrell would walk in trepidation to his door, where their knock was answered with the words 'I am the Devil's master'. People consulted him about life, love and ailments, but it seems that cursing and lifting curses were his speciality. One story tells how a girl was brought to him barking like a dog after being cursed by a gypsy woman. Taking some of the girl's hair, her nail parings, blood and urine, he placed them in a 'witch bottle' and boiled them up until the bottle exploded. Thus the curse was lifted and the charred remnants of a woman's body were found in a nearby country lane the following day. As he grew old, Murrell predicted the precise date of his death – 15 December 1860 – and sure enough he died on that very day.

17 December **Leechcraft and Cures of Essex Cunning Folk**
In 1903 the practice of 'Blessing the Geese' in Epping was recorded in *Folklore Record*. The rite, which was much in demand in the area, was carried out by Mother Jenkins. She drove the flock of goslings out of a lane on to a stretch of grass at the roadside and then walked round them spreading her arms over them and waving a little stick as she muttered her incantation, bowing to right and left as she did so. The 'blessing' was firmly believed to ensure the flock would grow up to be 'healthy and flourishing'.

18 December **1931** The rear wagons of a goods train heading for Thurrock became separated from the rest of the train owing to a defective coupling but the driver, unaware of this, drove on as the loose wagons gradually came to a standstill. The guard in the rear van was expecting a stop in the area, and would have had no reason to be suspicious, especially as dense fog had reduced his visibility to only a few yards. Soon afterwards another train came steaming along the same line, and its driver did not see the lost carriages until it was too late. Two people were killed in the collision, including the unfortunate guard, who probably had no idea what hit him.

The Drunkard's Cloak.

19 December **Old Punishments – The Drunkard's Cloak or Spanish Mantle**
Excessive drinking and unruly drunken behaviour are nothing new. Between the sixteenth and eighteenth centuries the judiciary employed a simple punishment

for their 'lager-louts'. The top and base of a barrel were removed, and holes cut in it for the arms, and the culprit was made to wear this awkward 'cloak'; a metal collar was then locked around the offender's neck, by which he was led around the town by a beadle or other official.

1848 Questions began to be raised about the curious 'coincidences' experienced by PC Charles Drake. He had been on the force at Dunmow for little more than two weeks when a series of mysterious fires occurred. Drake was always on the scene first, and had even passed an odd comment to fellow PC Amos Coote that policemen 'had a wonderful chance to set fire to anything if they had a mind to'. Members of the public reported their concerns when they saw Drake early on the scene at other fires and heard him say how much 'he liked to see a good blaze'. Eventually the circumstantial evidence was so overwhelming that Drake was charged with arson. He was acquitted on the judge's instruction but was dismissed from the force in May 1849.

1827 John Turner (alias Harris or Newman) was executed at Springfield. He was the leader of a gang of thieves that operated in the Runwell area and had eventually been brought to justice after a robbery at Ramsden Crays. The judge deferred sentence on three members of the gang until the last day of the Assizes. Two were saved from the gallows, but in his address to Turner his lordship was relentless: 'It is clearly to be seen that you are head of a terrible gang and justice demands that you should be made an example of. So numerous have been the depredations of late in this county as to render it almost impossible to dwell in; and while you are suffered to go at large the sword of justice will be wielded in vain.' The judge then placed the black cap on his head and sentenced Turner to the ultimate penalty of the law.

Old Punishments: The Crank or Teaser
The crank was a widely adopted means of occupying prisoners within the 'Separate System' in British prisons during the latter half of the nineteenth century. In Springfield Gaol, Chelmsford, the crank was known as the 'Teaser'. As in most prisons, it was used to occupy prisoners in their solitary cells. Operated by a single prisoner, the crank comprised a drum on a metal pillar or a handle set into a wall with a gyrometer (or 'tell-tale') to register the number of times the crank handle had been

The crank.

turned – usually about 20 times a minute, a typical target being a total of 10,000 revolutions in 8½ hours. If the target was not achieved in time, the prisoner was given no food until the dial registered the required total. An interesting legacy of the crank remains today: if the prisoner found the task too easy or behaved obstreperously, the prison warder would come and adjust the screw, making the handle harder to turn – hence the prison parlance for prison warder has, for generations, been 'the screw'.

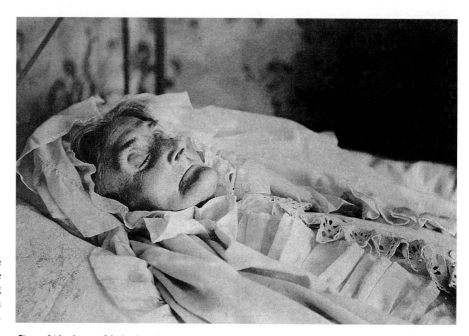

An example of the Victorian vogue of photographing deceased relatives in their coffin.

23 DECEMBER **Essex Witches and Witchcraft**
Eliza Vaughan, the daughter of the vicar of Finchingfield (who was installed at the parish in 1864), recorded the tale of a local woman who was suspected of being a witch. When the woman died her relatives had her laid out in the coffin downstairs and were beginning to sort through her effects upstairs when they came upon a box containing 'strange little things'. Suspecting they might be imps, they threw them on the fire. When they returned downstairs to pay their final respects, all they found was a coffin with a heap of ashes in it.

24 DECEMBER **1830** James Ewen and Thomas Bateman were executed at Springfield Gaol. Ewen had been found guilty of setting fire to a barn and stack belonging to Mr Sach at Rayleigh, but he swore his innocence to the end. The evidence against him was very tenuous, and he had been implicated principally by a man named Richardson, who had been convicted of being an accessory to the crime. Bateman had been convicted of highway robbery and the attempted murder of an elderly man at Lindsell. He had stamped the old man's head into a ditch, tearing off his ear (it was found in the mud

afterwards). They were executed in front of a large crowd. When the rope was placed around Ewen's neck, Bateman was heard to exclaim, 'It's a tight fit.' Ewen ignored the remark but turned to one of the officials and said, 'It's rather cold standing up here.' After the necessary preparations were made they were both launched into eternity.

Merry Christmas, Spider. The Bear Hotel in Stock is a fine old English inn. Its greatest character lived in the nineteenth century and was an ostler named Charlie Marshall, known to his friends as 'Spider'. If you stood him an evening's drinks or offered a wager he would crawl up the chimney in one bar and come down the chimney in the other. If he was feeling particularly coy, he would stay up there until a fire was lit to drive him down again. One Christmas Day, perhaps after too much feasting, he attempted his usual feat and scrambled up one chimney. His audience waited and waited, and even lit fires, but Spider never came down again. His well-cured remains are said to be somewhere in the pub's chimneys to this day.

25 DECEMBER

1856 The home of Barnabas Wrigglesworth, an elderly resident of Ramsden Bellhouse, was broken into and a great deal of property, including a pistol, was stolen. Two men, Elijah Ramsey (26) and John Cutting (50), were spotted about 6 miles from the burgled house on the morning after the robbery carrying large bundles. Inspector Howard went to a pub in Mucking, where he found Cutting asleep in the stable. Rousing the sleeping man, the inspector demanded a search and immediately found a greatcoat belonging to Mr Wrigglesworth, in the pockets of which were quite a number of the stolen articles. Luckily Howard was alert and he noticed Cutting slip his hand into his pocket; suspecting the worst, he seized his hand and his suspicions were confirmed as he controlled the removal of a loaded pistol from Cutting's pocket. Restraining his suspect, the inspector also found a black veil, no doubt used for the purpose of disguise. The accomplice, Ramsey, was found at Cutting's cottage in Grays Thurrock, where the rest of the loot was recovered. When brought before the Assizes their defence was weak – they claimed to have bought the items – and both were found guilty. They were revealed to be incorrigible rogues: there were five other indictments for burglary against them, and Ramsey had previously been sentenced to fifteen years' transportation. Both men were then sentenced to twenty years' transportation.

26 DECEMBER

1677 Buried in Romford on this day was Charles Salter, a tanner of South Weald, who had received a blow on the head 'whereupon hee dyed', delivered by one William Peake, a member of the town's Watch.

27 DECEMBER

1864 This day saw the public execution of Francis Wane, the 'Chadwell Heath Murderer', at Springfield Gaol. Wane had lived with Amelia Blunt for some years, until she tired of his drunken 'ill-use' of her; fed up with his 'lamentable ignorance' and resentful of the fact that he sent her

28 DECEMBER

out to work, Amelia walked out and went to live with an elderly man named Warren, to whom she was soon engaged to be married. Wane was heard to utter repeated threats that the marriage would never take place. Watching the rear of her home in Dagenham, Wane waited until Amelia went to the outside wash-house alone and while she was washing he crept up behind her and cut her throat. A prime suspect for the foul deed, Wane was almost immediately taken into custody. The evidence was soon assembled and the jury at his trial was so convinced they almost immediately returned the guilty verdict. Instantly Wane confessed to his heinous crime and resigned himself to his fate. On the morning of his execution, he thanked the prison officials, calmly shook their hands and, despite having deformed feet, mounted the scaffold without assistance. He was observed to 'die almost instantly when the drop fell'. The considerable crowd assembled to watch the execution 'conducted themselves in the most orderly and decorous manner'.

29 December   **Essex Witches and Witchcraft**
All manner of curious charms were used to ward off the malign attention of witches. Among those judged most effective were 'witch bottles' or 'witch jugs', such as the small grey jug found under a house being demolished in Saffron Walden in 1852, while another dug up from some old foundations contained the typical contents of thorns, horseshoe nails, water or urine. Two mummified cats were also found on either side of a chimney in the Crown at Wormingford in the early 1980s. It is believed these poor animals were walled up alive to provide psychic protection for the building. Their bodies were dated to about 1600 – a time when local woman Elizabeth Newman was tried for practising witchcraft.

30 December   **Grim Tales of Essex**
Alfred Marden was involved with some of the most significant cases investigated by the Essex Constabulary, from the shooting of Inspector Simmons (see 18 May) to the Moat Farm Murder (*see* 14 July), but in 1912 he was disciplined on various charges dating back to 1903; they included the unorthodox questioning of prisoners, using foul language and being disrespectful towards his senior officers. He was punished with a reduction in rank from superintendent to inspector. He resigned shortly afterwards. In December 1920 he appeared again at Grays magistrates' court charged with asserting he was still a police officer. When he persisted in doing so, he was threatened with a further reduction in his pension.

31 December   **New Year's Eve**
The last night of the year has always been a time for tall tales and shaggy dog stories – in this case, literally! Shane's Shaggy Dog was a spectral hound which was once said to walk between the entrance gates of Crix House on the Chelmsford side of Hatfield Peverel. The beast was quite benign until one day a startled carter hit the dog with his whip and was struck by a bolt of lightning. Shane's Shaggy Dog was seen infrequently in the years afterwards,

Inspector Alfred Marden.*(Essex Police Museum)*

until one day it tentatively made an appearance when one of the first motor cars in Essex happened to be passing the gates – so shocked was the poor hound that it spontaneously burst into a ball of flames and was never seen again.

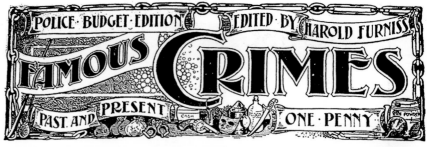

DOUGAL IN THE DOCK AT SAFFRON WALDEN POLICE COURT.

Vol. II. No. 25.

Samuel Dougal, the notorious Moat Farm murder, in the dock. He was executed at Springfield Gaol, Chelmsford, 14 July 1903.

Essex Executions, 1865-1953

Ferdinand Edward Karl Köhl: 26 January 1865: *Last Public Execution in Essex*
Michael Campbell: 24 April 1871
Richard Coates: 29 March 1875
Charles Revell: 29 July 1878
James Lee (aka Menson and Adams): 18 May 1885
Joseph Morley: 21 November 1887
George Sargeant: 15 August 1888
Thomas Sadler: 18 August 1891
John Davis: 16 August 1893
James Canham Read: 4 December 1894: *The Southend Murderer*
William Wilkes: 19 July 1898
Samuel Crozier: 5 December 1899
William Burrett: 3 October 1900
Charles Howell: 7 July 1903
Samuel Herbert Dougal: 14 July 1903: *The Moat Farm Murderer*
Bernard White: 1 December 1903
Richard Buckham: 4 December 1906
Frederick Foreman: 14 July 1910
George Newton: 31 January 1911
William Charles Adolphus Beal: 10 December 1912
Charles Frembd: 4 November 1914: *The last man executed in Essex and the oldest person to be hanged in the twentieth century.*

Subsequent executions for murders committed in Essex were mostly carried out at Pentonville Prison, London. The locations of exceptions are given in brackets:

Johannes Mommers: 27 July 1926
Hashankhan Scamander: 2 November 1926
Frederick Guy Browne: 31 May 1928: *The Murder of PC Gutteridge*
William Henry Kennedy: 31 May 1928 (Wandsworth): *The Murder of PC Gutteridge*
Robert James Kirby: 11 October 1933
William Turner: 2 January 1943
J.C. Leatherberry: 16 March 1944 (Shepton Mallet): *The Taxi-Cab Murder*
James McNichol: 21 December 1945
John Riley Young: 21 December 1945
George James Newland: 23 December 1953

ACKNOWLEDGEMENTS

It has been proved, yet again, that you meet some of the nicest people when researching the grimmest tales! In my travels researching this book I have met many helpful and interesting people. There are, sadly, too many to mention them all by name, but I wish to record my specific thanks first and foremost to Sarah Ward at the Essex Police Museum, who generously and enthusiastically assisted my research there. I also extend my gratitude to Stewart P. Evans, James Nice, Dr Stephen Cherry, Peter Collins, the Revd David Gilmore, curate of the parish church of St John the Baptist, Danbury, the Revd David Kirkwood, St Mary the Virgin, Little Parndon, Yvonne Branson, churchwarden at St Mary's Runwell, Michael Fountain, Colin and Rachel Stonebridge, Essex Tourism, the staff at Essex Police Headquarters, Colchester Castle Museum, Saffron Walden Museum and the University of East Anglia Library, and the library staff in the local studies sections at Halstead, Colchester and Saffron Walden, and Essex Record Office.

'All contributions gratefully received.'

Sincere thanks, as ever, are due to Terry Burchell for his photographic wonders and to the editorial staff and graphic designers at Sutton Publishing. Every attempt has been made to contact the owners of copyright for images used in this book. If any omission has been made it is not deliberate and no offence was intended. All the pictures are taken from the author's archives unless credited otherwise. The modern photographs of monuments and gravestones were taken in Essex by the author during the last five years.

Last, but by no means least, I thank my family for their continuing love, support and forbearance of this temperamental author.